SAND
and
STARS

SAND
and
STARS

MISSIONARY ADVENTURE

ON THE JUNGLE TRAIL

Ruth Stull

....

FLEMING H. REVELL COMPANY

CONTENTS

FOREWORD

Born of Americans whose ancestral roots ran deep in French-German and Scotch-Irish soil, and transplanted for years of missionary service into a veritable botanical paradise in the interior jungles of Peru, where every branch of the fanlike Amazon bears a different name, I now write of the people I have met and the life I have known. My story is of Christian adventure, in which of necessity I had to keep my feet in the sand while my heart was in the stars.

Childhood in Ohio hills, schooling above the Hudson's palisades and foreign assignments among volcanic peaks, have been parts of a divine pattern. Normal levels, tragic depths, ethereal heights—all belong to that moving mural of life which can appear less than wonderful only when one has waywardly or unwittingly missed his place in the design.

Life on earth is of the sand, but only one step short of life celestial. I want *Sand and Stars* to help readers straighten themselves, lift their hearts, open their eyes, enjoy the sun and at times when darkness falls see rainbows in the storm and night's diamonds in the dark.

R. S.

Mansfield, Ohio

7

SAND
and
STARS

And the angel of the Lord
called unto Abraham . . . and said . . .
I will multiply thy seed as the
stars of the heaven, and as the
sand which is upon the sea shore . . .
and in thy seed shall all the
nations of the earth be blessed;
because thou hast obeyed my voice.

GENESIS 22:15–18

Now to Abraham and his seed
were the promises made . . .
And if ye be Christ's, then ye
are Abraham's seed, and heirs
according to the promise.

GALATIANS 3:16, 29

STARLIGHT

FATHER INTENDED me to be a boy. He already had two daughters, but my failure to be the son he had planned did not alter the relationship he had decided upon for me. From my earliest childhood I spent much time with him as he read. I remember him in just two occupations, working and reading. He did not play. Hunting was his recreation.

As the city did not provide experiences he thought essential to children who would be adults in a little while, father took his family to a big house at the top of a rocky glen where we could see spring become summer, and summer mature into autumn. Treasured experiences of my childhood took place out there.

During these summers I was taught the things of soil, fields, woods, winds and rains. Father taught me to use his guns, command his dogs, and ride his horses. He wanted me to know about Blue Jack, whose mother, Dolly, the beautiful chestnut-sorrel was loved by all of us. I cringed in speechless fear for her that morning in the stable. When her offspring tried his uncertain legs for the first time, he seemed to think

11

he had been given the wrong set. They were extra long, and decidedly too wobbly to support his sleek body—a body beautiful, and so shining that when he took a few hesitant steps across the velvety grass, the summer sky was mirrored on his coat.

I knew that the strong, graceful animal frolicking across the length of the meadow on legs which quickly learned to serve their purpose, belonged not only to Dolly but to the stallion whose flesh quivered like the ripples on Silver Lake when he approached the chestnut-sorrel—our Silver Lake, at the end of the pasture where the horses drank, and where we sailed weed pods for miniature boats, and fished for minnows.

During childhood I arrived at such understanding of spiritual things as was suggested by the oil paintings in the immense velvet-bound album of sacred pictures in the family library, by people I knew. In one picture two children chased butterflies dangerously near the edge of a cliff, and were safe because a guardian angel hovered over them. Good people were pictured on the pages of the big book, and I knew some good people. My grandfather Taylor prayed briefly when he visited us, with a slight whistle in his prayer that was missing from his ordinary speech. I regarded him as very good. He walked with a crutch I supposed he had been born with. It had, however, been with him only since the Spanish-American War. He never complained about it. He did not lean on it, but wore it as a knight wears his armor.

Grandfather Taylor was good company. Games were not necessary when he came, for his talk was all the entertainment any household could wish. It was our highest privilege to enter the dining room on Grandfather Taylor's arm. At the top of Lookout Mountain, in a museum where war trophies are displayed, I many years later turned the heavy pages of a great book and found the name of Thomas E. Taylor listed with other heroes. I treasure his memory.

When a very little girl I stood at the garden gate of the home in the country and watched a tall old man with white hair herd cattle along the roadway. He carried a tall staff, and looked like the Abraham on the pictures in the library. I did not know that when I was smaller he had laid his hand on my head and said to my mother, "This girl will be special. She is your unusual child." My parents called him "Mr. Constance." In my thinking he could have been Abraham—or maybe he was God. Did not the pictures show the Good Shepherd with a staff herding sheep? This could be God herding cattle. I never asked anyone. In any case, the old man seemed to have been given an insight into my future.

God was not well known to me. I understood that the world was His, and that one day it would end. That did not seem reasonable, for the world was wonderful. It would be a waste to let it be destroyed in a sudden cataclysm, yet I thought that was to be.

One autumn morning when mother was getting me ready for school she told me to look at the brilliant coloring of the trees in the woods, for in just a little while it would be gone. She meant only that winter would blow autumn away, but invisible fingers of fear closed over my heart, for I thought it was to be the end of the world.

I had been properly churched, and given all the benefits of the sacred rites. Firm foundations, the faith of our fathers, and the march of Christian soldiers were known in song and pageant, but I had no knowledge of a fortress for my soul. I did not know what the faith of our fathers was, and I saw no reason for a Christian to wage any warfare. The social life, however, was satisfying and I accepted that as the primary purpose of the church.

After a while my parents began to hunger for spiritual food. They seemed to sense that the cupboard of their inner lives was bare. Surely the abundant material life they knew could not be all there was for a man made in the image of God! There must be an inner peace, an equipment for the invisible life, even as seedtime and harvest provide for the physical. Mother would lean forward week after week in her pew eagerly awaiting her minister's next sentence, hoping that he was going to tell her how peace could come to her soul and her house. But he never did.

Then the Reverend L. H. Ziemer, a minister in our city, found the truth of God's plan to live aboundingly in the life of the believer and, fired with renewed zeal, began to declare what to him was fresh truth. Eager listeners followed his simple instructions. They experienced peace transcending circumstances, power for victory in the hour of temptation, energy for usefulness in the world. All my family entered into this new way of life—all but me.

My family was wonderfully changed. They were like new people. I enjoyed their quiet radiance, but could not be persuaded to investigate the source of their new interests nor to associate with their new acquaintances. To make it possible for me to meet them, a group came for an evening in our home.

The minister and a number of friends talked for a while, Scripture was read, and finally everyone bowed in prayer. A very broad statement was made seeming to indicate, as I understood it, that everyone who wanted to spend eternity in heaven should lift his hand. Of course I wanted that, and lifted my hand. Then the minister stood by me, placed a heavy hand on my head, and prayed what seemed to me an awful prayer, for he ended with, "and the God of all grace, who hath called us unto his eternal glory by Christ Jesus, after that ye have suffered a while, make you perfect, stablish, strengthen, settle you." I wanted heaven some time, but not now. Nor did I want to suffer, be perfected, stablished, or settled. I wanted none of that, and for two years I avoided all these people except my family.

The swirl of social life was increasingly exhilarating—then suddenly it was over—a war broke into our sparkling fun. A train stopped in our city, and when it rolled on our men went with it. We were bereft more than we knew, but it was no time for tears. Rather it was a time to devise ways to live without the love we missed—time to work and to wait—for men who perhaps would not come back. Girls met in public buildings to roll bandages and daydream of absent lovers. Until now my life had been filled with sunshine; gladness met me at every turn in the road. The strands of the rent fabric of that pleasurable life were never woven together again.

The heartaches and losses of war alert leaders to the need of spiritual ministries, and a city-wide evangelistic campaign was held in an immense temporary auditorium. Like practically everyone else, I attended some sessions, but felt no response to anything I saw or heard.

Several young men dropped into our downtown recreation spot, and in something of a spirit of challenge suggested that the young attendant of the place bring his pal to the evening service. It would be a sporting thing to do, so the two young men-about-town went. They had no idea of becoming interested, but after that they attended of their own accord. On their way to one of these services Ross Stull told his pal that they must sit down front, as he was going to accept the invitation to become a Christian. Both of them knelt at the altar of prayer, and arose knowing that their lives had been changed and were to be expended for God.

Ross immediately associated himself with a group of Christians, and attempted to be useful in his new way of life. He realized readily that he had no adequate knowledge of the Word of God or of the way of prayer, and wisely sought a school where he could be taught. That fall he went to New York.

He studied not only books but men, and became closely associated with the founder of the school—one of the world's eminent Christians, A. B. Simpson. One day when he had taken the doctor to an important meeting, and had helped the elderly man to the platform, the great missionary leader said to him, "My boy, it takes a hundred men to make a pin. The success of today's ministry will be credited to you." This revealed one of his traits of true greatness.

Ross had a spicy sense of humor, a good tenor voice, and throughout his school years sang in male quartets. While home on vacation he addressed an audience of his townspeople, and out of respect for my mother's request I attended that meeting. He saw me in the audience and was attracted to me. He did not know my name, nor did he meet me until two weeks later.

At first our friendship was based on conversations about spiritual matters of which I knew little. He was not preachy or threatening, but acquainted me with a way of life that surpassed the most fanciful tales I had ever read, and the most colorful opera I had seen. In every fiber of his slim, tall body he was enjoying a life that was not only physical but spiritual. In his pocket was a small Testament. In it he showed me the prescription for those fine qualities I discerned in him. His personality was not an accident, but the result of a divine Personality dwelling in his heart. His assurance of success and satisfaction in things future were based on a faith that made those things actual instead of potential. The little book explained them. They were not things he had trumped up. Many people knew about them. I had just kept away from such people.

My first session with Ross pointed me to another way of life. It was not that he talked of high or deep spiritual spheres to be explored; rather he was an album of choice productions from such explorations. My lighter way of living for things visible, tangible and present was not condemned; it was simply acknowledged as of this world's best, but entirely of the present world. From the accepted facts of history, and the statements of inspired Scripture, the world at its best could be but a thing of time and vanity. Investments in it, and expenditures on it, would be consumed with the using. With the dawning of eternity the world with its systems, visible charms and mental prides, would pass into oblivion—only he who had done the will of God would abide forever.

My whole existence had been based on the present world —its offers, satisfactions, accomplishments, pleasures. He did not suggest that I was bad; he seemed to know that I was not. He simply said that I was missing something that he had found to be good.

Before the summer ended I had heard the principal contents of the sacred Scripture. I was persuaded at least intellectually that the best of living is known only to those who employ the Bible formula for it. I had always known that God had made the world and the people in it. Now it seemed reasonable to believe that His rules for the people He had made would be best.

Alone in my room, I knelt, strangely conscious of the presence of God, accepted His Son as my personal Saviour and His Book as the guide of my life. The following night I found a public altar where I openly confessed what I believed in my heart.

A sparkling gladness entered my life. It was perhaps comparable to that of an orphan who suddenly is adopted by wealthy and loving parents. I belonged to God's family, for I was accepted in His Son. While I continued to walk the sands of earth, my name was written in a book above the stars. I was registered. Now the thought of the world ending or eternity dawning was only that it would be another phase of a life already possessed.

Daily occupations took on new importance. Now a day well lived, dollars earned, acquaintances made, were all part of something that would not pass away, for they were turned into the bettering of my life and that of others—an endless investment. My desire to serve the God who had given me life and salvation left me baffled, for I had no power with which to honor Him. There was a prescription for this condition also in the little book, and my young guide found it. I was to know the presence of the Spirit of God occupying all of my yielded life, but I feared complete yieldedness, thinking that God might want me to go somewhere or do something I would not desire. After hours of rebellion, I at length arrived at a willingness for any place or anything. Then I recognized a Presence in my life as of God being there. This Presence has never left.

New thinking, quickened living and a quiet depth of contentment became the order of my life. I felt neither conquered nor subdued, but wonderfully liberated and invigorated. That I must resign my office position gave me no regret. I would serve the God who first had given me natural life, and now eternal life through faith in His Son. I had little knowledge of the Word, but I would study it. I would enter school at the opening of the fall term. I cashed the bonds in which my savings had been invested to secure money for transportation to New York and instruction there.

My spiritual life developed under the tutoring of the guide who spent hours with me. Our evenings were delightful, whether alone or in the company of others. The entertainment and activities of the new circle of friends were different but fascinating. There was rightness, interest and fun. Stars blinked out on the night Ross first told me he loved me. He had been a high priest in my thinking. He had introduced me to things spiritual, and under his guidance I had become new-born and enlightened, concerned about things eternal. Ross wanted an engagement. At Christmas I gave him my promise in the words of the Bible, "And Ruth said, Intreat me not to leave thee, or to return from following after thee; for whither thou goest, I will go; and where thou lodgest, I will lodge; thy people shall be my people, and thy God my God: where thou diest, will I die, and there will I be buried: the Lord do so to me, and more also, if ought but death part thee and me." I cared for no one else. He was the star that had risen to light my life and fill my heart. He had guided me to eternal life and I owed him my life if he wanted it. He did. Our blended hearts were to know much more of starlight than I could then have anticipated.

The year after Ross completed his studies, I also graduated. Fourteen months later we were married—married by the minister who had placed his hand on my head while he prayed that I be made perfect, after that I should suffer a while, be established . . . settled.

The next day we drove away into the South to take up our work together. After twenty-one months in Florida, Ross Orville Stull, now an ordained minister, became the pastor of a city church in Dayton, Ohio. Here his work was promising and effective, and I shared in the responsibilities as I had in the South. He encouraged me to take part not only in the community work but on the platform also.

JUNGLE CALL

AFTER THREE years in Dayton we were led, providentially I believe, to attend a missionary conference. Ray B. Clark, a Britisher who had been one of three explorers sent to survey a wild territory roamed by the Campa Indians of the Amazon Valley in Peru, was reporting his findings.

Though I had never been conscious of any call to the foreign mission field, I immediately became greatly interested in his description of those Campa Indians. According to his story, they lived in the distant interior, three thousand miles up river from the mouth of the Amazon. No one had ever taken the Gospel to them; it is doubtful indeed that they had seen many white faces. They were hostile, and still lived in the bone-and stone-age manner of their fathers. They were not even subject to governmental control. But they were a numerous tribe, scattered throughout the length and breadth of a primitive tropical forest in the lowlands east of the Andes, ten degrees south of the equator, where the mighty river is but a handful of creek-like beginnings. Someone, the speaker insisted, should go to them, win their confidence, and teach them the Way of Life. He quoted a verse of Scripture which says that Christians should go into all the world and preach the Gospel to every nation. He called it the Great Commission.

For several days during the twenty-minute missionary session I listened to this kind of talk. Then Damascus light and Macedonean vision struck me together—a settled conviction that I was one of those who should go. In fact, I had an inner compulsion to go at once. But I happened to be a minister's wife, and could scarcely leap to my feet and start trekking off to the Amazon jungles, to teach the wives of red men.

But, strange to say, almost simultaneously Ross felt that he must go too, but he did not talk about it for there were many problems involved—things that pull hard on the heart strings—fathers, mothers, houses, lands. The explorer had reported that where the Campas lived there would be no roads on which to drive a car, no houses in which to live, and no conveniences of any kind—just a vast jungle filled with neglected red men.

Pencil sketches in our note books registered our interest. Mine were of campfires, tepees, feathers; Ross's of miles, dollars, tribes-people and years. Then we talked about it. It seemed logical to believe that since there was a Lord of the harvest, it was His prerogative to summon workers into His fields. He had summoned both of us; of that we were sure. So when we returned to our church that eventful August we immediately resigned our charge, announcing to the people that we had volunteered at the missionary conference to undertake the evangelization of the Campa Indians in Peru. Children cried. Young people pleaded to go with us. Older folks pronounced blessing upon us. To eliminate the possibility of a change of mind, we immediately put practically everything we possessed up for sale. We could use the money for our proposed plunge into the jungles. Doctor Ziemer, the man who prayed so ominously when I was young, and later had performed our marriage ceremony, was now pastor of our home church at Mansfield. He telegraphed that the church would provide our transportation and first year's support on the field.

My husband, a minister now turned missionary, set out for New York to discover how he should go about reducing an unwritten language to writing. At the same time I entered a hospital for training as a resident nurse, in order to be helpful in a part of the world where there would be no clinics, medical aids, doctors or nurses. After five months we again joined forces and set out for South America.

We sailed on the S.S. *San Cristobal* from New York to the Canal Zone, where we had an agreeable wait of a few days, and received a foretaste of what life was to be like in the far south. Even now the fragrance of ripe limes, the perfume of gardenias, and the clatter of sandals flapping on cobble-stone streets remain with me. There we were first introduced to staggering crabs with their funny eyes extended on something that looked like pipe cleaners. We traveled in old carriages drawn by thin horses along flower-bordered avenues where oleanders swung low to brush our heads. It was all new, and our hearts were young. Just to know that we were nearing our field of service made us glad.

The trip across the Panama Canal proved both educational and interesting. From our first contact the captain befriended us. Frequently he would invite us to be his guests on the bridge where we could get a better view of the operation of the lifts and locks, and observe the jumping fish.

At Buenaventura, the port city of Colombia, we transferred to an Italian vessel which lay in port from one high tide to the next. Now we were in South America! In a little rowboat at the wharf lay what appeared to be an immense beef liver. Actually it was a sting ray. A fisherman informed me that its lance-like tail could strike anguish into its victims, and at times death. Little did I imagine at the time that only a few years later I would be cutting a three-inch length of the saw-toothed lance of a sting ray from the leg of a Campa Indian!

Out on the Pacific, which totally belied its name, I suddenly became disinterested in eating. Like a fabled predecessor, I at first was afraid I would die; a little later I feared I would not! When at length I ventured into the dining room I saw on the table what appeared to be chilled cantaloupe. Upon investigation, however, it proved to be luke-warm papaya, in my condition not only tasteless but nauseous. I developed so pronounced an aversion to the fruit that when I arrived on the field, I felt that our fellow workers could not be quite truthful when they said they enjoyed it.

Though we had volunteered for work in Peru, mission policy required a certain quota of new workers for Ecuador before more could be sent elsewhere in South America. So we went to Ecuador in anticipation that it would be our door to Peru. At once we became enchanted with the land and its people. For two months we remained in Guayaquil, the port city, and studied Spanish. It was a novel experience. No matter how poorly we spoke their tongue, the natives assured us that they understood perfectly, in fact, we spoke it better than they did. Whether this was technique, psychology or mere flattery it served to encourage the newcomer to talk.

Breakfasts in Ecuador are something special. There is no change in menu—quantities of fresh tropical fruits, hard-crusted bread baked in the morning and brought through the streets with its fragrance announcing the hour, orange marmalade, and *cafe con leche*. This last is the delicious hot milk flavored with the essence of coffee, which a kitchen girl with patient skill prepares. The coffee is roasted to a rich dark hue, powdered, pressed into a fine sieve where boiling water is very slowly dripped through it. This essence of coffee is added to boiled milk as cream is added to coffee in North America.

From the coast we were sent to Quito on the equator. Years would be time too brief to explore everything there. My mind is rich with the beauty I saw and the intrigue of life and legend learned from the people whose home it is.

Ambato, half way between Guayaquil on the coast and Quito on the equator, is called the land of the eternal spring-time. We were stationed there for eighteen months, and would gladly have remained there. A revolution hemmed us into this place for three months when the railroad tracks below and above the city were torn up and turned back, and the enemy armies lined the ridges of mountains that wall the basin where the city lies. Patriotism is violent, and the demonstrations we witnessed were revealing and shocking. A handsome young officer wrapped the Ecuadorian flag about him, and stabbed himself through its colors. We were safe under the protection of the Stars and Stripes which floated over our mission house, and watched the bloody drama with senses tingling.

Revolution effects rapid changes in status. The doctor with whom I shared a case in the hospital where one of our missionaries was a patient became the president of the republic several days later.

Ambato was without salt so long that when the first train brought burlap bags of dirty rock salt, a riot ensued as people fought for possession of it. I got refined salt by refining it myself. A native woman taught me how to do this. I put the dirty crystalline chunks in an earthen vessel and covered them with water. The next day the entire content of the jar looked like dirty water. I strained it through muslin and boiled the liquid. Much of my work was done in those days with a book of Spanish verbs in one hand. The language had to be thoroughly learned, and oral and written examinations passed, to the satisfaction of the mission authorities on the field. This day a wooden spoon was in my other hand, for the moment comes as salt solution is boiled when suddenly the heavy pan is minus liquid, and white salt as if by magic, fluffs in its place. It must be quickly, energetically and constantly stirred until thoroughly dry. I felt like a magician every time I accomplished this amazing test, but the native woman who was alternating her memorizing of Scripture verses with my trying out verbs on her, seemed to consider the refining of salt only an act of ordinary routine.

While living in this dreamy mountain city we witnessed the panic of terrified people calling upon their saints as they ran into the streets from houses they feared would crush them when a slight tremor shook the place. Earthquakes that had never hurt Ambato—Ambato that has since been devastated beyond recognition—Ambato that is being rebuilt by people who belong to it, and who do not think it will ever again be destroyed.

The satisfying accomplishment of conducting a mission in this city was interrupted when I fell a victim of typhoid fever. Stark dread filled my husband's heart, for the bubonic plague was laying the city low, and residents could not travel out of it without a doctor's permit. Under cover of darkness a native pastor helped him put me into a hired car, and he drove through the night over mountain roads to Quito, where adequate care could be given me.

Ross stayed by my side night and day, leaving only when the doctor commanded him to. Then he would walk the streets, pray, trust and wait. The doctor asked his permission to bring interns to study my case. This might help others in similar circumstances.

During the days and nights preceding the crisis of the twenty-first day, I talked to my husband of things not earthly. It seemed as if I were speaking to him from another world. He later confessed that he scarcely dared touch me for fear he might complete my translation. The beautiful relationship which existed between us became even more sacred during those nights of borderland communion.

When recovery came, we returned to Ambato and shared the work that had been taken care of by the national pastor during our absence. Then came a cablegram from the chairman of our mission in Peru stating that they needed us there, and that he had word from the New York Board to the effect that we would be immediately transferred if we requested it. We acted promptly, for we had come to South America to work among the Campa Indians in Peru.

Ecuador by now had won our hearts, and we had to wrench our affections from numerous interests. Snowy mountain peaks in the distance, our rose garden that blossomed every month of the year, the rosy purple of the banana blossom, the people of Ecuador—these had taken their places in my life, though I had known none of them before my arrival there. Then there were the children of our missionaries. We had borrowed the tiny tots and returned them only when we had to. We had clothed them and fed them, but always had to go through the heartbreaking experience of giving them back when the new baby was old enough for brother or sister to come home, or when the parents returned from itineration.

When we left Ecuador our own baby was on the way, and I could not go at once to the jungle. My husband would have to go, and I would manage somehow—we both were confident of that. I stayed with Mr. and Mrs. George P. Simmonds, wonderful new friends in Lima.

The night before Ross left to be absent five months, my host with his deep bass voice sang,

> I'll be loving you always.
>
> .　.　.　.　.　.　.
>
> Not for just a year, but always.*

* Copyright, 1925, Irving Berlin.

My heart nearly broke, for if ever I needed my husband's helping hand it was then. But I knew it was right, and the singer was only trying to entertain us. He did not know I was all tender inside, and that my tears were about to drown out his song.

Friendships were plentiful on the coast. The teachers from the high school of another mission board, and the doctors and nurses from the British-American clinic, were friends of my hosts and we spent many enjoyable evenings in good fun and fellowship together. During those months of waiting I made a layette, and prepared for the child that would be F. David Stull.

One month before our son's birth my husband returned from the jungle, a thin but enthusiastic man. He had discovered that a white man could live in the jungle and decided a woman and a baby could, too. We would all go in when our son was old enough.

A number of doctors and nurses had supper with us one night in the cozy little house we had rented when my husband returned from the jungle. Mr. Clark lived with us. After an evening of fellowship the guests went on duty at the hospital, and later in the night we pinned a note on the guest-room door informing the occupant that we were going to the hospital; he could look us up there in the morning.

In the low, white-walled Spanish building that was the British-American clinic at Bella Vista my husband placed a kiss on my lips and a string of pearls in my hands, and informed me I had given him a son.

When later I left the clinic, I found our house lavishly decorated with roses, Martha Washington geraniums, and hibiscus. A little Spanish maid had been secured who proved to be a gem of efficiency. It was this Senida who remembered each Wednesday to open the floodgate at the front curb to admit the water from the irrigation system so that our flowers and lawn would not wither and perish. It does not rain there, but melted snow from the mountain slopes keeps Lima's gardens beautiful.

Life was pleasant, exciting and entertaining in this scenic metropolis near the Pacific coast. When we drove from the port city of Callao to Lima, thirty minutes farther inland, we followed a new highway. Ever since leaving New York I had beheld new and startling sights, but I was really shocked to see a skeleton sitting on the porch of a house along this highway. The road had just been cut through an immense mound that was an old Inca burial mountain. Many levels of burial had been cut through and bones were scattered along the roadway. But to sit on a porch was not standard conduct for a skeleton, and signs were posted the next day forbidding the collecting of bones and trophies along the road. The remaining Inca descendants had objected to this type of souvenir gathering.

Mingled feelings of amusement and excitement tumbled about in my heart when I read the letter in the afternoon's mail from the mountains. Ray Clark was now the field chairman for our mission; he traveled up and down Peru to superintend the work in various areas. He was going to marry a girl who had come out from the States, and who was teaching in Huanuco, high in the Andes. Travel is costly and difficult, and affairs of the heart have to fit into field duties. Ray and Marian decided that while he was up there on this official assignment they should announce their engagement.

The letter beside my plate at the dinner table asked me to buy an engagement ring, have announcements printed, and send all the necessary material to Huanuco as quickly as possible. My little Spanish Senida knew how to scoop señorita clams from their shells and make the most delicious chowder ever tasted, and over the results of her good cooking I pondered the selecting of a ring for the happy lovers. Ray's letter told me I would know what kind of ring she should have. This was no easy assignment, but evidently I did all right, for their marriage has lasted through the years, and they are continuing their fine work in Lima now.

Lima is unforgettably lovely in much that is older and much that is more modern than in most of our cities. When David was five months old and it was time to start the last lap of our journey to the Campas, we found our hearts tied in with the life of the people on the coast. There were many friends and interests from which we must separate. We had received new missionaries from the homeland and had seen them off to their various places of assignment. We liked our work in the coast city, but we said good-by to the pretty house in Miraflores, which means see-the-flowers, and is the part of Lima where it is very nice to live.

Senida wept and pled with her mother to permit her to go with us—Senida, who knew how to dainty my room the way I liked it, and who loved our baby. She had accepted our faith and did not want to be separated from us. But she was strictly forbidden ever to mention the subject again, for her mother was certain these North Americans would be killed, and so would she if she went. According to folks on the coast, we were going to sacrifice ourselves to savages who would never permit us to enter their territory. Another party from the coast had tried it some years before, and all of them had been killed. Missionaries of other boards frankly stated that they considered the venture risky, too.

THE TRAIL

WE DEPARTED from Lima on a train that leaves sea level at eight o'clock in the morning, and attains an altitude of over sixteen thousand feet by three o'clock in the afternoon. I was glad the government doctor watched the passengers and applied oxygen when our baby wilted like a little flower. Adults have died in their attempt to make this trip.

The train goes only one day's journey. From there we traveled on fascinating but dangerous mountain roads in a light truck. The driver knew the danger and so did each passenger, but it was the only way to get on, so we did not discuss the matter. I really appreciated the heights and depths, and was concerned only about my baby. But he stood the two days of car travel better than any of us, for I scarcely put him down, and constantly clinging arms made for pleasant sleeping.

The mountain hotel at the end of the road offered rest and food, but I felt too weary to eat. I wanted only to lie down and rest. George Simmonds, our host during the waiting days on the coast, had graciously come this far with us. To morrow he would return to his family, but he was trying to get us off to a good start. He came up from the hotel dining room with a bowl of hot chicken broth and insisted that no matter how I felt, I needed it, and should take every bit. He was right. A little later I went down and had the rest of the meal, in fact felt quite normal again. My baby was laughing; all of us were unhurt. The only fault I ever pinned on George Simmonds was the "Always" episode. The Simmondses and I laughed about it when I saw them in Los Angeles a while ago.

From here on we would ride mules over a trail etched along the mountain sides by government men. The back door of a revolutionary republic is very important, and Iquitos over on the Amazon is Peru's back door. There was only this way to get men or mail from Lima, the capital near the west coast, to Iquitos east of the Andes and east of the jungles where Peru touches the waterways of Ecuador, Colombia and Brazil.

Few passengers ever cross the trail, but it is kept barely usable, and at the end of each day's journey a man with his household is stationed to keep a fire burning, and to provide meager entertainment for the carrier of the mail and such passengers as go that way.

Ray continued on with us. When we took to the trail in the morning, I considered it a bit humiliating that I was mounted on a mule instead of a horse. For mules are like some people I have known; they simply cannot be managed. You do not guide them; you simply go along where they are going. Later I learned that it was government rules which put me aboard a mule; they did not allow horses on the trail. So I rode a mule; that is I rode him off and on. On one occasion in wriggling his way up a rocky ascent, he crawled right through the saddle bands and left me on the trail, still in the saddle. Nothing was damaged except my pride, but I con-

sidered the episode far less comical than did my two companions.

As far as those gentlemen professed to know, it had never
been done that way before. And while they considered it some
sort of precedent, they advised me in the future to apply a bit
of leg work and try to stay with my mount. In spite of the
best of intentions I could not always manage it.

My mule was tall and slender, and I really developed a
liking for him before our days of sojourning together were
over. It was really not his fault when he stepped off a ledge,
fell on his sturdy neck, and plunged me pell mell over his head
into a sea of sticky clay. Fortunately I landed on my feet, and
my companions, seeing that I was unhurt and perfectly capable of resuming my throne in the saddle unassisted, forgot all
about Sir Walter Raleigh, and remained on their mounts
where they could better enjoy the performance. Thus they
missed a plaster of Paris suit like mine which the hot sun
malevolently baked on me.

I did manage to stay with my mount when, wearied of
stepping over the ridges made between the troughs by a string
of cargo mules to form a Jacob's Ladder, he gathered his four
feet together on the top of a ridge, and leaped rabbit fashion
from one to another. That was most unsettling, and I certainly
was glad when he decided to change both his method and
mood.

I never seemed to be able to change that mule's mind
about anything; I just had to try to understand how he meant
things. One day I wanted very much to persuade him against
his will, but learned never to attempt it again. It was one of
those poetic mornings when birds dip low to pronounce the
earth good. A mountain stream had provided a natural shower
bath for us as its refreshing waters dashed over us at a little
falls. In high spirits we had set out for eleven hours of riding
on the trail. The keeper of the government post where we

spent the night volunteered the news that before we reached a similar post at the end of that day we would come to a condemned bridge. We might be able to cross it, as the last he had heard it was still standing, but under no circumstances were we to permit two mules to be on it at the same time.

As soon as we saw the bridge we recognized it, and could only marvel that it had not already gone down the stream. It was the low swinging type, made of small poles cut from slender trees and woven together with vines—more hammock than viaduct. However, we were glad it was still there, for in South America there is no way of estimating when a repair job will end; we could have been delayed for weeks even if repairs had already started. Ray crossed first, while Ross waited obediently, holding our son in a canvas basket on the saddle in front of him. A feather pillow in the basket suspended by straps from daddy's shoulders preserved the wee one in reasonable comfort.

The mule on which I rode was white and a good follower —too good, in fact. For when the black one bearing Ross and David started across, he immediately decided to follow. Almost frozen with terror, I whirled him around with all my might. I would teach him that he must not cross that bridge until I let him. Then that mule got mad, awfully mad, and started back over the trail we had come at a speed of which I did not think him capable. He was through; that I understood perfectly, and the only thing left for me to do was to try some mule psychology. So with tender coaxing that bordered very closely on endearments, I turned him again and let him choose his own pace, but in the right direction.

Nor was the matter ended. For upon reaching the bridge again, I saw that the other mule was only about three-quarters of the way over. As if in devout meditation, he was still picking his steps cautiously along the swaying and heaving length of poles. Nevertheless, by this time I knew my mule was boss;

I wanted no further argument with him. So I just closed my eyes reverently, and adjusted my motions to his jerky steps, as he stamped onto the bridge with little snorts as reminders that he was still displeased. He was determined to catch up with the lead mule, no matter what the cost. When at length the sound of the other mule on the bridge vanished, I opened my eyes, assured by the faith that comes from sight that I would complete the transit safely.

All of us carried long poles with sharpened tips which were useful in many ways. On one of these days on the trail I got myself into another jam when I tried to hurry my husband's mule just ahead of me by prodding him with the pole. Ray had managed to speed up his charge, round one of the many hairpin curves, and was just across the gorge from us. But my husband's mule decided that he was in no particular hurry, nor was he in a mood to be hurried. Instead, he reared up on his front legs and flayed the air with a lightning-speed kicking of his hind legs. My husband! Our baby! Already I could see them hurled into that seemingly bottomless gorge over the edge of the shelf-like trail. When the mule felt that he had sufficiently expressed himself, he selected a gait to his liking and moved slowly forward. Our friend across the gorge laughed heartily at this circus act, suggesting that we ought to charge admission.

As each day ended I was more and more thankful that I would not have to travel back over that trail again for some years at least, for it turned out to be far harder than I expected. In fact, at the end of the first day I rather childishly complained to my husband, "You knew it was like this, and yet you brought me!" It did not seem to me that I could make another day's trip. But I did. I discovered that a woman can be quite rugged if she has to be.

Behind us was a string of twenty cargo mules, bearing our baggage and supplies. Before starting out the Spanish muleteer had direfully warned us that we should under no circumstances let these cargo mules catch up with us. Where the trail was not solid rock they would trample it into such muddiness that we could scarcely use it. To prevent this, we started two hours ahead of them each morning.

One day our mules misstepped into the clay and were thrown. Time had to be taken out for the mending of saddle bands and other repairs, which delayed us so long that the cargo train caught up with us. When I heard the tinkling of the warning bell on the lead mule, I was naturally afraid. As quickly as possible we flattened ourselves against the mountain wall and watched breathlessly while the string of mules with their bulging loads passed us like a freight train. Since they knew that they would drop their burden at the end of the day's trail, and there would find pasture, they wished to lose no time. I was grateful for that tinkling bell for it would not have been a pleasant experience to have been caught on the outer edge of the narrow trail and be pushed off by these sturdy beasts.

Once I saw the foot of that mule ahead—the one which carried the most precious things to me in all the world, my husband and our small son—as it slipped on the edge of the cliff and dislodged a piece of rock which went tumbling down and down, my heart going down with it. It was what could happen to that mule ahead that put a tightness around my heart.

One morning—it was Sunday—the way seemed too difficult, the heights too high and the depths too deep. On my face were tears and in my heart a sob. At that moment my heavenly Father sent a green cloud of tiny parakeets from the mountain peak which flew boldly out over the canyon in utter defiance of its awful depths. They did something to me, way down inside, with their brilliant feathers flashing under the sun, and their merry chirpings filling the air with song. Had not my

Lord declared that each of us is worth more than many little birds? Soon I was again at rest.

Our frightened mules snorted and braced themselves as we rounded a bend of the mountain, and suddenly came upon an enormous snake lying in the sun against the mountain side. Soon after, at the bottom of the descent, we came to a river with no bridge over it. It was only after much persuasion that our mounts entered the water and waded across to the other side.

Because of repeated delays, we failed to reach the government post where we had planned to stay that night, and darkness overtook us on the trail. Travel in the dark was doubly perilous, especially when we were high in the mountains with a river flowing in the valley below. So often did I feel my mule slip and flounder under me and hear the lunging of the mule ahead, that it seemed I could stand it no longer. To attempt to direct the mules was useless, for they knew far better than we where the edge of the trail was. For my encouragement my husband, riding ahead, would call back over his shoulder some of the precious promises from Holy Writ he knew so well. So dark was it that I could not even see the white ears of the mule I was riding, but from the Scriptures I could sense the perfect safety of those who trust in God.

There was much confusion around the campfire as we emerged from the darkness and moved off the muddy trail. Strange to say, the cargo mules that had passed us were not being unloaded. Stiff from the long journey, it was with considerable difficulty that we dismounted, but when we did, it was only to be told by the little inn-keeper that we could not remain for the night.

Oh! We must stay! That made no difference; we were told we simply would have to move on. There was only one guest room, which already had been engaged by three young students from a European University, who were members of an expedition collecting rare butterflies. It had been their plan to continue along the trail too, but the wildness of the mountains which made travel so difficult persuaded them that their collection of butterflies was sufficiently extensive and they were heading back to civilization.

If we had only been chasing butterflies, we doubtless would have turned back, too. But we were commissioned, and a commission is not lightly to be discarded, particularly when it has come from the King of kings.

Ours was a quest for the souls of men. God had entrusted to our hands a message. We were to take it at whatever cost to those who were ignorant of it, who did not want it, who might even reject it barbarously. But their souls and ours were of equal value to the Creator. The difference was only in the pigmentation of the skin—plus circumstances. So the hardness of the trail must not dissuade us. We must find the Campas, and we must deliver our message. It meant the difference between life and death, eternal life and death, to the Indians.

Quite definitely we could not tarry at the camp that night. The three young men rightfully had prior claims on the premises. To our suggestion that we be permitted to make camp with our sleeping bags and blankets, and sleep outside by the fire, the keeper of the inn said, "No." For, he continued, we would probably lose some member of our party to a leopard—then he would lose his job with the government. The emphasis was distinctly on his job—not us.

So that was that. We could not sleep out of doors, and there was no room for us in the palm shelter. This added up to the obvious; we would just have to go on. As I turned slowly back to the mule from which I had dismounted with such difficulty, my muscular soreness seemed to have increased in geometric progression. It was a little too much for my emotions.

Instead of climbing up into the saddle, my head fell down

on it and I did a distinctively feminine thing—I cried. I know
that missionaries are not supposed to shed tears, at least not
over themselves, but tears do work miracles, as every man
knows, and those did. For the spokesman of the three students
stepped gallantly forward to protest that the lady must not be
permitted to attempt another lap of the journey; they would
relinquish their room to us. I had read Emily Post; I had also
been taught that an offer of such a sacrificial nature should be
refused, at least the first time it was extended, but on this occasion I brushed aside all amenities. I just tumbled into bed,
leaving the young men to climb into the loft. Soon I was to
discover that this was filled with rice straw, for they moved
about during the night just enough to keep us under a sneezing
shower of rice and chaff. But I was thankful even for the
chaff—anything but that muddy, slippery trail in the darkness.

To all of us it was a miserable night. The only light in
our room flickered in from the campfire outside and inter-
mittently from our flashlights. As his bed for the night I had
tied baby's basket to one of the supporting poles of the hay
loft. Over the basket we tucked a mosquito net to keep out
such inquisitive callers as spiders, mosquitoes and cockroaches,
for the place seemed literally to be on wheels, or more exactly,
legs.

Suddenly out of the darkness two bright spotlights
beamed at me from the doorpost. They might have been almost anything. These were unusual accommodations; they
accommodated almost everything. For instance, in addition to
the guest room, and the corner where the keeper stayed, there
was a lean-to separated from us by a slight split-palm wall.
That room sheltered a herd of swine, and we definitely knew
they were there. Beyond them in the woods we could hear
leopards with their hungry coughs all through the night. But
so long as the pigs were there, so the keeper had assured us,

we need have no fear. For the leopards, with their rare powers of discrimination, would select them instead of us.

But those bright spots on the doorposts—I must call my husband's attention to them. He investigated and discovered that they were the eyes of a tarantula, an immense banana spider. Needless to say he exterminated it, and before the morning six more like it. The eighth one spent the night taking his daily dozen on the pole to which baby's basket was tied. After observing his gyrations for a while, I satisfied myself that the tarantula was not seeking white babies to devour; he was merely doing some scientific research on cockroaches. When the tarantula approached a roach, that member of the order *Orthoptera* in pure terror would release his hold and drop. That was the explanation of our planetary display of cockroaches throughout the night. The eighth spider was spared not because of his superior virtues, but because I feared that if smitten he might land in my sleeping bag. To see him up there at least brought me a degree of assurance.

While my husband was feeling around in the dark for something with which to kill the tarantulas, he picked up outside our door a long slender package which a carrier had removed from one of our cargo mules. Several days later when he happened to open it, he found inside a small white cross, a useful little device to be set up alongside the trail as a marker where a traveler had plunged over the edge. As I jogged along, those little wayside crosses had caught my attention, and I had peeked over the edge of the precipice a number of times to see them. Once, twice, or even three times a day, we would come across one of those markers. The small scattering of bleached bones below, and the bits of strap and metal, told their own tragic story. How easy it would be to plunge down and join that number and be remembered henceforth only by a little white cross.

It is not to be wondered at that during the first night on the trail the question came to my mind, "Shall I go on, or shall I go back?" After all, nobody was pushing us. Our Board in New York had not insisted that we go. There were other places where we could work. I thought back over the day just past. The trail had been so treacherous that to push on and risk seven more days of it seemed to be more than I could take.

Then I began to pray and in turn listen to my Father's voice. Out in that palm shelter, under such wild conditions and circumstances, He whispered to me that He knew all about this trail and this crawling, howling jungle mountain. He had known all about it even before He had asked me to go. But with His commission went His promise, "Go, and lo I am with you alway." It was enough. I would go on. I would not be afraid.

When morning came, strength returned and my soul revived. The rising sun was beautiful; gaudy parrots chattered; baby cooed; everthing was fresh and good. God was recharging us with courage and faith, and causing us to see that while the trail was hard it had its compensations. Some days we would ride for hours on a path carpeted with tiny pink and white stars and orchid bells which had drifted from overhanging trees. They filled the air with sweetest perfume. Again we would ride beneath the fronds of giant ferns, while the banks alongside were covered with deep moss, and edged with white violets.

Large clear-blue butterflies darted about us in the sunshine. Here was lavish beauty at its best—primordial creation unspoiled by the trample of the Adamic race. Upon rounding a cliff, a mountain would lift its head beyond the river like a huge tapestry dangled from heaven's balcony, patterned with scarlet, orange and purple against green. In silent wonder we worshiped the Artist who alone could perfect such a design; we adored the God of creation.

Mountain trail was succeeded by water. We felt that to reach the river where we could transfer from mule-back into a dugout would be to put one foot in heaven. In fact, it proved both easier and harder. Out in the open the sun beat down mercilessly, and we burned under its direct rays and from the reflected heat. Fortunately I had purchased a paper umbrella from a Chinese merchant in a little oriental shop while I was in San Cristobal, Canal Zone, and now the investment began to pay off. The dugouts were larger, heavier and broader than birch-bark canoes, but they were of the species canoe nevertheless. With our cargo in them they were weighted heavily. As we moved along, the current was strong and whenever the canoe would get a little out of control, it would take in water and almost toss me out. We were a long way from home, and I wanted to lose neither my possessions, family nor life.

At the end of our first day on the river we arrived at the camp of a half-breed which was located on the river's edge. Like most of the people we were to meet in the jungles, he had a story. His father had come from Europe to get beyond the reach of the long arm of the law; his mother had been an Indian; but both were dead. The only hospitality he could extend us was the privilege of sleeping on the porch, for there was but one room to his house, and that had previously been engaged by a cow which he had been able to acquire only after great difficulty. He could take no chance on losing it to the leopards. While we were getting our sleeping pockets ready for the night, he tried to cover his apparent discourtesy by telling us of a leopard's visit soon after he had obtained a much coveted dog. He had a shotgun for protection, and the Indians working with him had bows and arrows, but these proved worthless, when in weariness only a few nights before they had all fallen asleep at one time. A leopard emerged from the forest and with lightning-like speed leaped over the half-breed, snatched up the dog, leaped over two Indians, and vanished into the night. They did not even get a crack at him, and they simply could not risk losing the cow. So we must sleep outside—not the cow. This bedtime story was not especially conducive to sleep, but tired bodies overcame anxious minds. At least by morning we knew a little more about the country in which we had come to live.

Leaving, we could discern no signs of human life; it was as if we were in an unpeopled world. For hours we would move along with no sign of smoke, and no sound of human voice. All was jungle.

We passed the mouth of the first branch river which emptied into the great Pichis, and when we came in sight of the mouth of the second river, we were at the place earlier selected for our mission post, our forest home. To scramble up over the river bank was for me a major accomplishment, for it was about two hundred feet high and sloped at something like a forty-five degree angle. I eventually made it by grasping the trunks of small trees, bracing a foot against a root, and sliding through the mud. Only one was there to welcome us. But there was jungle—unconquerable, wild, rugged. And we had arrived. Now for that life in the open which in childhood we had coveted. But this one was real and permanent, with split bamboo instead of canvas walls, and palm leaves for a roof. Of course we knew it would be like this, and we cheerfully accepted the situation. Were we not together, husband, baby and I? We would manage. We would learn to like it. We would cause the jungle to respond with a living sufficient for us. We would win for Christ and to ourselves the Indians living there. We would reach for the stars, even while struggling through the sands.

JUNGLE

WE LIVE anywhere as nearly as possible as we would live anywhere else. To do this, when North American urbanites determine to transfer themselves to a South American jungle, they must not only do the things which come to them naturally, but also develop their latent creative and imaginative powers. True, the lure of new experiences and unexplored places will fan the passion for discovery and stimulate the mind into unwonted activity, but these can never obviate the need for supplying the basic necessities of life.

Water for instance is a vital project. In North America water ordinarily is merely something to turn on and off with a cunning little spigot, but in the jungles it has to be caught as it falls from the skies, or snatched from the river before it flows past.

With our impedimenta was a little white enamel tub, an omnibus implement for which we had cause to render many thanks. Now, when there was no baby in it, we set it out in the open where it might implore the open skies, then receive the answer to its prayer. Kitchen pots and pans served in the same manner. These vessels were evidently theologically minded, for they received the second blessing. In the morning not only did we find priceless water in the utensils, but numerous winged creatures floating on the surface. Black lacy-winged things they were, with minute ruby-like dots to mark the point where a fragile wing was delicately hinged to a slim body. Some had a bar of emerald or amethyst across a wing. And there were edgings of gold on deep-green velvet moths, and silver filigree on purple beetles. This novel reservoir held for inspection each morning more beautiful things than are to be seen in many museum galleries.

There was no water in the jungle ground; there were no springs, no wells. Of course a whole river full flowed right past our door, at some seasons crystal clear, but often clogged with logs, stumps and decayed wood materials. And there was this drawback when we thought of drinking—the river afforded a convenient, moderate-priced cemetery for the tribe. It was a wonderful river, however, and since flowing waters have a way of purifying themselves every few feet, this did not constitute too great an obstacle. While the death rate among the Indians is high, the forest is so vast, and the population so scattered, that the ill effects from this burial custom are not so serious as might at first appear.

The river was entrancingly beautiful and I loved it. Though I lived on its banks for almost a decade, I never grew tired of looking at it. Every morning it would don a fresh dress, and every evening a different gown. It was constantly changing each time we looked—more blue, gray or purple, smoother or rougher, with clouds which mirrored the open sky by day, and at night tied a silver ribbon from the moon around its waist. Planetaria exhibit far less beautiful displays, yet to this one I had an orchestra seat, and that free of charge, right beyond my campfire.

A school of fish. like a dark cloud many feet wide and

hours long, went up river to furnish bushels of fresh fish for
the many jungle fires. For fishing the Indians especially grew
barbasco. They would pull up the twisted, slim roots of the
small shrub by hand, crush them between heavy stones, and
cast them into the river. So powerful was the narcotic thus
formed that the fish would turn turtle and play possum. The
Indians, looking rather like well-browned fish themselves,
would leap into the river, catch the floaters in their hands,
hold them between their teeth, swim to the river's edge, and
fling them on the grass for women to gather into baskets along
shore.

When asked if the eating of these fish was not dangerous,
the Indians would explain that the fish were not poisoned, but
stunned. "Leave them alone," they told us, "and they will
swim away again." We found that was true. This root has
now gone into mass production, and is shipped into the States
under the name of *cube*, where it is used to add punch to certain insecticides.

So many and varied were the species of fish that swam
our river that we are sure we never saw all of them. Some were
playful, others vicious. On several occasions we watched while
a whale-like spouter accompanied his aqueous display with a
strange barking sound. The Peruvian rivers are the habitat of
various savage fish which travel in swarming hordes and devour the bodies of men and beasts alike. When in unbelievably
short time the swarming fish dart away, only a bare skeleton
of their victim remains.

Electric eels hang out their "Fish at Work" signs in certain lengths of the river. The red men know the danger spots,
but at times in order to assert their bravery, or to impress some
coquetish squaw, they venture a swim at these places. Those
who succeed are immediately acclaimed kin to the sun god.
The oldest son of one of our Indians was killed in a bravado
act of this kind. He was snipped by an eel, and by the time a

rescuer was able to reach him he was dead, whether from shock or drowning they did not know. I saw the younger brother of this victim receive the severest punishment at the hands of his high-spirited father that I ever saw administered to any Indian boy. The father literally lacerated with jungle nettles the entire surface of his son's bare body with a whipping which would be remembered for many stinging days. The father did not intend to be cruel; he merely wanted to guard against losing another son to the eels through venturesomeness.

At a certain season of the year a white sand bar appeared above the surface of the river. It did not look so much as if the river was falling as that the sand bar was lifting its head above it. Mother Nature had scrubbed its surface white, while the stones which studded it sparkled like diamonds. We would paddle out to it, walk on it, even swim around it when it seemed safe. One day as we watched, a leopard stepped out on the opposite bank of the river, then swam to the sand bar. There he proudly put his tawny body on display in the sunlight, pausing only to sniff disdainfully in our direction. He seemed to have no appetite for human flesh that day, and soon retired once more into the woods on the other side. None of us complained about his decision.

Another day, as we were putting along upstream in our launch, a leopard leaped from a tree which had fallen into the water, and swam out to midstream as if to attack our boat. My husband jerked his rifle to his shoulder, but the big cat experienced a change of mind, swam back to the river's edge, climbed aboard a log, and then slunk away into the leafy jungle. It was a splendid performance.

Even the natives make no attempt to rid the jungle of wild animals or snakes; there are far too many of them. They just try to protect themselves as best they can.

On another occasion a lazy alligator which was sunning

himself contentedly on the river banks, suddenly stirred his great length, whipped his tail, plunged into the water, and approached our dugout. We knew that just one swish of his heavy tail could write finis to our whole story. So Ross took careful aim, and we got him before he was near enough to strike the dugout.

Every river trip has its thrills, with new dangers and delights at almost every turn. When traveling near the bank we might hear our red men's warning cry, "Look up, look up," and as we obeyed we would see a boa constrictor stretched along the branch of an overhanging tree. It is a favorite sport of these reptiles to wait for a small animal to seek a drink at the river, then stealthily extend themselves a link or two and invite the little fellow into their dining room. When one of our friends shot a boa, he discovered that the serpent had swallowed a whole deer, horns and all. After such a full-course dinner, the boa coils himself up like a refrigerating system, layer on layer, leaving only his ugly head to protrude from the top of the heap. With an air that all's right with the world, he just suns himself for several days while his meal digests. There is no need to worry about a well-fed boa.

Quite unintentionally, I assure you, I stepped on a snake one day. It was not a boa, but to me plenty large and hideous. It was completely hidden among ferns where I was searching for some rare plants with which to fill the hanging baskets my Indian women had woven for me. As frightened as myself, it slid from beneath my boot and writhed its way down to the river. For some days I lost my interest in ferns, and was downright mad that a serpent had invaded my Eden. But later I ventured into the deeply-vined places again; I guess rare plants intrigued me more than slimy snakes angered me.

Always we entertained the captain of the launch when he had time to stop with us. In appreciation of the courtesy, he kept on the lookout for some gifts he might bring—a string of

onions, garlic cloves, a bag of coffee beans, a mold of hard
brown sugar, a great pod of Brazil nuts as they came from
the tree, dried fish not known on our river, and other simple
but to us collectors' items. The good captain was our friend,
but he fell a victim to the hazards that characterized his calling. To our deep sorrow he was drowned when his launch
struck a floating tree and sank. Never so much as his bones
could be found. The Pichis river is a cruel treacherous water-
way which makes no attempt to honor its victims.

That no object which sank beneath its surface at cur-
rent-filled places would ever be seen again was traditional
among the Indians. My husband tried to disprove this theory
by shooting a deer in midstream. So dearly did the Indians love
the white man that they would have worshiped him after
they became Christians if he had not forbidden it. If the white
man wanted to test their time-honored theory, they would
help him test it. So after the shooting, they searched the river
diligently for two whole days, but they could find no trace
of the animal. Their theory still stood.

The sand bar grew peanuts as if it was a nursery. Few
edibles reach maturity in jungle land without constantly
fighting for life against the attacks of vicious enemies, but
peanuts were an exception. The only trouble was that they
seemed to prefer life on the sand bar. We had produced an
excellent crop, and tomorrow would come the harvest.
Virnatta, a peanut specialist if ever there was one, had been
placed in charge of the fabaceous herbs. She had planted
them, with parental eye had watched them grow, and tomorrow would harvest them. Then lightning struck. During the
night the river rose to a majestic height which completely
submerged the island, in fact covered it so deeply that it did
not reappear for a whole year. Thus were our precious peanuts buried in a watery grave, without benefit even of a com-
mittal service.

If ever there was one, that was a day to weep. But the rainy season was at hand and there would be tears aplenty from the skies for days on end, so I deemed it foolish to add to the precipitation. But to forestall a similar disaster, we decided to plant a little earlier next year, and thus harvest a little sooner. One lesson the pioneer must learn is that no single battle makes a war. He must be wiser next time and beat the force that hurt him. Eventually he will conquer if spirit and body persevere. Of course we had peanuts the next year—lots of them—big fat ones. I roasted them in an iron skillet, shaking and stirring them all the while. Then I rubbed them between towels and tossed them into the air so that the wind might separate the skins from the nuts. How good they were! My cut-glass bowl, an anniversary gift from friends in Ecuador, was filled with them many times over.

Life at the jungle post was never monotonous; it both fascinated and threatened. Constantly it went to extremes. Night enclosed me with my thoughts, and I enjoyed that, but night also brought the fluttering heavy-bodied bird which whirled out of the dark to the ground near my fire, where it screamed as if a thing possessed. I wondered whether it were bird or demon. Then there was that seemingly incessant threatening cough of the prowling leopard seeking prey.

On these nights I would tuck the little pink blanket a bit more closely about my baby, and lift my heart to God in prayer. Then He would bring to my mind the language of the ninety-first Psalm: "Thou shalt not be afraid for the terror by night," and I would turn to the twelfth chapter of Isaiah, there to find an answer for my trembling heart. Soon it became easy to say, "Thank you, Father; I will trust and not be afraid." In the field of day-by-day experience we proved that the secret place of the Most High is truly under the shadow of the Almighty. We learned to say with perfect tranquility of heart, "He is my Refuge and my fortress; my God; in him will I trust."

Too, there were other campfires beyond ours—strange campfires—from which painted redskins emerged with death-dealing bows and arrows. Fear rode with them, and again I would have to run to God. Then He would point me to the rest of His command for the night, "Thou shalt not fear for the terror by night; nor for the arrow that flieth by day." Up to then I had seen in that verse only a promise, but now He gave it to me in the form of a command, as firmly as though He should say, "Thou shalt not bear false witness." Previously "fiery darts of the wicked one" had been figurative arrows, but now they were literal ones. Again my heart declared, "I will trust and not be afraid," and sleep would come.

This was truly a land of adventure, where white men often sacrificed their lives in an attempt to conquer the wilds. The jungles of Peru are primitive forests of immense trees and densely foliaged undergrowth such as characterize the regions lying near the equator. The stretches inhabited by the Indian tribes are immense, and appear to be sparsely populated even though there are many forest dwellers. The jungle is in fact a great land mass of silent forests, silent rivers, silent trees. You may travel for hours without hearing a sound except that of nature, unless it be the rhythmic dipping of your own paddles.

There are just two kinds of jungle nights. One is when there is no sound at all: then the stillness is so thick you can feel it. On such nights it seems as though all nature has gone to bed, and when nature sleeps all is quiet. The things which mark civilization are nonexistent. There is no train or trolley, auto or carriage, factory or pavement. Nature sleeps and the world is at rest.

But those nights are few, for the average jungle night is alive with sound. Beasts and birds, insects and reptiles compete to win first prize as noise-makers. The sounds are weird, terrifying. In all the bedlam there is but one sound which in any wise approximates that of civilization. This one resembles the roar and rumble of a train in the distance, but you learn to identify it with the coto (goiter) monkey which is howling at the edge of your clearing.

Farther in the jungle the quiet is more rudely disturbed by the sounds of tribal life, as the Indians gather near a circle of campfires in a clearing to celebrate the return of the full moon. This they do in indescribably heathenish dance and revelry. Beneath these forest trees primitive savagery continues as it began ages ago. Indeed there has been nothing to change it, for even the advance agents of civilization have never touched these people. Their god has continued his benevolences to them day after day. They can do no more than follow his example—rise, shine, and set, for the sun is their god. And it should be stated, the setting far outshines the rising.

The red men are unchanged; they are primitive; they worship a half-time god. They are children of the forest. They spend their lives under the trees, but the trees do not tell them of salvation. They gaze meditatively into the sparkling waters of their rivers, but those rivers do not sing of a Saviour. They mark their directions by the stars which lay highways of light across their rivers, but those stars do not guide them to heaven. They date the passing of time by the moon, but that moon does not reveal to them a God who shines on when life is past. Nor have they any trustworthy plan of salvation. The way to God and heaven must be explained to them by lips of witnesses sent with the message of peace.

We had gone to this wild distant place for only that purpose, to teach them the way of God. But the problem was, how could we get these red men to listen to our story?

It was useless to inform them that we had come to preach

the truths of the Bible, for the Bible had no meaning to them. They had never seen a printed page; they employed no system of writing. We must simply tell the story, but we must first win them to ourselves in order to get them to listen.

So the missionary went fishing with the man of the forest. While the Indian stood in his canoe and shot arrows into the fish as they flashed near the water's surface, and gathered in his arrows as they floated down the river to him, the white man dropped his line over the edge of the canoe and hauled in his catch.

The man of the forest immediately became greatly interested in the fishhook, and was told that he could have one if he would come along to the white man's camp. Upon arrival, a fire had to be kindled, and the Indian's interest in a fishhook was succeeded by his enthusiasm over this modern convenience, a match. When the white man produced a frying pan, the Indian sat back in deep wonder, watching the marvelous performance at the campfire. Of course by then it was dark—the missionary had planned it that way. Since it was too late for the red man to return to his fire up river, he stayed all night. Before the fire died down and the red man slept, he had listened to a story which so gripped his heart that all the novelties in the mechanical world he had seen seemed trivial in comparison.

He remained the next day and the next. By that time he began to sense something of a new power stirring his heart, an urge not to cruelty and hate, but to submission and peace. Soon he returned home, constructed a raft of balsa logs, and floated his entire family down to the mission clearing—all in order that they, too, might hear this wonderful story, that they too might feel the pull of this power of peace.

When his friends heard about the benefits of association with the white man, they came too. And with the coming of each family the clearing increased, for each added his little clearing to ours. Soon there was a large clearing and many Indians. The jungle gradually was being pushed back and many friendly fireside circles established.

Since time around the fires was insufficient to tell them all they wanted to hear, classes of regular instruction were started. This was the beginning of a Bible school—a school established near that river which was the jungle highway.

RED MEN

W E HAD crossed swinging bridges, climbed towering mountains, and traveled treacherous rivers to reach the abode of the Campas, and now that we were there we could neither talk nor understand their tongue. We would have to learn it as any primitive, unwritten language is learned. English meant nothing except to Ross and me. We had studied Spanish for use on the coast, in the mountains, and for government requirements, but it would seldom be needed in the interior.

Hardly had we lighted our campfire in the jungle before a dugout nosed its way onto the river's bank, and discharged an Indian who spoke Spanish. He was the only product of inter-tribal parentage we ever found in all our years in the jungle. His father was a Campa and his mother an Amueixa. The father, a high-spirited outlaw of his tribe, not only took a wife from an enemy tribe, but made his way down the branch rivers to take balls of raw rubber to trade with the rubber-gatherers on the big river a thousand miles downstream. Through these contacts the Indian and his young son

Miguel learned Spanish. Now Miguel, a grown man, had come ashore to discover what were the intentions of the white folks who were making their camp in his forest.

When the chief of the Campa tribe dies, his son does not necessarily succeed him, but rather the man with the most persons under his direct control. Consequently every man wants all the wives he can have, all the children possible, all the orphans, and all the unattached persons who can be added to his personal campfire circle.

Miguel intended to be chief when Vaca left office. He discovered that he could speak the white man's language, and proceeded to capitalize on that accomplishment in order to enhance his value and importance.

Miguel befriended the white man and never left him. He taught us how to fish as the red man does it—taught us to hunt the wild hog without being devoured by the herd before getting in a shot—taught us to give the call of the mate to attract the proud black bird called the *paujil*, which corresponds to our North American turkey. He taught us the language of the beetles.

One night he dropped by to inform us that we would not be taking our trip up the Apuruquiali the next morning. We told him that we must go, for the itineration was planned, our things were packed, the sleeping bags rolled, food prepared, and it was our desire to go. He insisted that the beetles were telling him there would be a tempest raging in the morning which would make it impossible for us to travel the river. His weather report was right; we did not leave the station the next day. A torrent of rain pounded against the surface of the river with such force as to send it up to meet the downpour. Wind and storm made river travel unthinkable.

But while the red man could teach us the language of the bugs, he could not teach us the language of either of the tribes with whom we wished to talk. His Spanish was good.

He understood everything I said and could answer me, but when I asked him to tell me how to say it in Campa, he would inform me, after at least pretending to think about it, that it could not be said in Campa. I knew it could, but I also knew that he would not be able to explain how. So I tried another way. I would say a sentence to him in Spanish and without exception he would repeat it to the nearest Campa. That was what I wanted. Then I would say what he had said to yet another Campa. If it was understood, it became vocabulary. If it brought no response, then I knew I had missed a sound or syllable, so later I would use precisely the same sentence and discover my mistake when Miguel repeated it. That is a slow way to learn a language, but it is a good way.

An old dugout came down the river, discharging seventeen bedraggled Indians with needs of various kinds. Some of them were sick; the side of a woman's head had been crushed by an angry man; a boy was snake-bitten; a daughter had been kidnapped and held by a vicious man. They all drooped in disheartened helplessness. There was much to be done for them.

Soon after their arrival at our place the mother of several of the young people in the group died and I decided it was a chance to get a girl to help me at my camp. Alcinda had not yet arrived to assist me, and I was doing all my work which included caring for my baby, learning two languages, and making a jungle produce home life for our family. To have an Indian girl help to keep my fire going, to bring me yuca root and peel it, to wash dishes, would be a godsend. She was perhaps sixteen years of age. But Miguel informed me that this was not a girl but a boy. Thinking he misunderstood which person I meant, I pointed again. Still he insisted that this was a young man.

It was easy to see how I made the mistake, for these youngsters all wore their hair just as it grew, except at the front where it was cut in long heavy bangs. These were fashioned by placing the hair over a log, then cutting it off with a sharp stone or bone. Bangs were the popular style for both men and women. Indeed, they served for more than style, for they created an effective screen to keep the gnats out of their eyes, making it possible for an Indian just to sit, and not have to sit and brush gnats. This suited him.

Men and women alike wore a long homespun and sleeveless garment called a *cushma*. These were woven and styled precisely alike except that the two lengths of cloth were sewed together lengthwise for the men and crosswise for the women. The beads worn as adornments were different, but apart from this they looked alike.

Miguel was right; my chosen girl was a man. I decided that some barbering for men would be a good idea. My husband told me that this was my tribe and that I could do with it as I pleased. By this time I had become quite efficient in cutting hair by practicing on my husband and our baby son. I have never known what inward misgiving Ross entertained when he allowed me to put clippers and shears to his hair for the first time. True, he had assured me many times that I could do no wrong, even when I felt he was simply employing a psychological approach to obtain what he wanted. But he really believed in me. And while I must confess that I was not proud of my first barbering, I at least recognized my mistakes and tried to improve on each subsequent occasion. Really, the poor fellow had no alternative. It was either necessary for him to let me do it, do it himself, or let it grow. He decided to let me do it.

When later a missionary couple, Frank and Viola Reifsnyder, came to work with us, the husband insisted that I also cut his hair. He simply knew his wife could not do it. But I blandly refused, arguing that she could do it just as well as I could, and that they would both be missing something important if she did not. I knew better what I meant than they did. Viola cut Frank's hair and soon was able to do it just as well as I. Neither of us would ever have touched shears to our husband's hair in the homeland, but out there we had to do it, and we did it fairly well.

But these Indian boys! Under a heavy bribe I got my girl-man to let me cut his hair. Then his brother volunteered and I barbered him. Then a dozen men wanted it done, but by this time my hand ached from the heavy cutting, and I told them I could do no more. But there was another way. If one of them was smart enough to observe how I did it, I would loan him my equipment and he could turn barber himself.

A bright-eyed young fellow quickly volunteered to accomplish on any head what he had seen me do. Of course he supposed that I had begun with my husband when he had been in the original long-haired state that was theirs. I had done well, but he could certainly do as well himself.

It was evening and they trooped into the interior to Miguel's campfire, where they usually went for any special talk or activity. With them they took my comb, shears and clippers, after I had supervised the ambitious barber on his first operation. His effort was successful, and I was glad to let him take over.

But next morning I needed the circle of my husband's arm, when at sunrise the Indians arrived, all of them shorn— clipped right down to their stubbly scalps. They had gone me one better. Maybe the white lady did not know you could cut it all off! They looked like so many convicts. I could not tell if my husband's motion against me was a sudden outbreak of petting, or laughter under a degree of control.

We both knew that no matter how grotesquely humorous might be the situation, there was inherent positive danger. For those heads had never been bared to the equatorial sun, and the heavy hair afforded protection as of a pith helmet. Suddenly their scalps were exposed so that the tropical sun would beat down upon the bases of their brains. We had seen sun exposure, and in every instance the afflicted Indian insisted that he had seen a ghost and would under no circumstances return to the place where he had been stricken. Days of lunacy followed in every case, with the afflicted ones ripping off their strait-jackets as fast as they were fastened on. They inflicted injury on themselves, and attempted to assault others. My head became light as I pictured these strong men turning maniacs before night.

We had never expected that we would be free from mistakes. But now, as on many occasions, we confessed to God that we had made a serious blunder, and implored supernatural intervention to cover our good intentions which had turned out wrong. After we had prayed, Ross assured me that I would at least make gentlemen of those who survived. We were humbly thankful when the shorn ones obeyed our instructions to stay in the shade for several days, and in the future to stick by the white man's way of cutting hair. Neither too much hair nor too little—that would be the plan henceforth. They got the idea, and today they are a well-groomed tribe.

The white man's hair-style pleased the Indian, and he decided that his way of dress should have like advantages. We had waited for this decision. The women of the tribe plant cotton; where they got the start we do not know. They keep the jungle pulled out from around their plants, and when the cotton is ready they spin it into thread by twirling it between their fingers onto a long thorn. The thorn is placed standing in a little pool of copal, a pitch-like substance extracted from the seeping wound of a tree. The pitch is held in a small ball over the coals until ready to drip, and then is melted onto the round flat stone that fits into the palm of the spinner's hand. After the copal hardens, the stone is spun in the palm of the hand, and the thorn receives the thread twirled onto it from the woman's other hand.

These human spinning-wheels do a beautiful piece of work, and with no houses to keep and little else to do, their time is largely occupied in making thread. When enough cotton is spun for two lengths of cloth, the loom is made from branches tied together with vines, a shuttle is smoothed from a piece of palm, and the homespun is eventually ready. Two lengths of it are sewed together, the woman using a thorn for her needle. She places the thread over the blunt end of the sharp thorn, drops a bit of copal from a heated wad on it, places a wet finger against it, and it is sealed—her needle is threaded. My way of putting the thread through the tiny eye of a needle seemed altogether unnecessary bother to them. Nevertheless, they came to acknowledge the advantages of my needles and used them efficiently later on.

These garments are dyed before being worn, as the natives do not like them white. They prefer brown, the color of the trees. From the bark of a tree they make dye by pulverizing it between two heavy stones. A little basin is dammed off at the side of the river, the brown powder is placed in it, and there the new garment is soaked for two days. Wash day never comes for the *cushma*. When the Indian thinks that something ought to be done about it, he prepares dye and colors it again. The garment becomes thicker and stiffer. When it finally wears out it is not because it has become threadbare or rips. Rather it wears off like old leather, breaking away from the bottom and top until it is up to the knees and down to the waist. Then it is time for weaving new cloth into a new garment.

To teach a school of seventy pupils was an ordeal, for each person had his own cloud of gnats hovering over him. I had to lean into the cloud to teach a man to write.

When the Indians suggested adopting the white man's

way of dress we sanctioned it, though we knew that would ruin the beauty of the tribe, for our clothing would not become them. They were far more picturesque in their own garments, adorned with nut shells, teeth of animals, beaks of birds, claws and feathers. They skinned small wild birds, sun-dried and sewed them to their dresses. They strung long bands of tiny nut shells, bones of animals and fish, or seeds of wild growths, and wore them diagonally over their shoulders. They were most attractive with their faces painted with the *achote*, a three-cornered red berry which they cultivated for the purpose. They powdered it between stones and made a paste by mixing it with fish or palm oil.

The men wore the red paint lavishly, but the women applied it in fine lines and artistic drawings. A woman would often express her mood with the design on her face. If she was merry she painted an arrow on her cheek to show that she would engage in conversation and be a friend to man. But if she was out of sorts, she would paint a black scorpion on her face, and that meant to keep out of her way, that she hated everyone and would strike if molested. It seemed an excellent plan!

The men worked for us and earned work-pants and shirts and loved them. The women soon wanted dresses, and I made many of them on my little machine which I operated by turning the wheel with my right hand while managing the cloth with my left. I taught the women to sew for themselves, and they became quite proficient. How proud they were of their garments!

Ross managed to make a foot-power appliance for my sewing machine, for which he constructed a cabinet that would have done credit to Singer. A strip of *sacha-vaca* (jungle cow) hide made a leather belt over the home-made wooden wheel, and then I really made time.

The best feature about the change in the clothing style

of the men and women was that with the adopting of our type of clothing they also employed our wash-day system. By keeping their new clothing clean, life took on an entirely different atmosphere, a sweetly different atmosphere.

New cloth was not used for a baby's or child's dress. Little things could always be made from the left-over pieces of a big garment which had been worn off from both ends. and that is how it was done. Stiff, hard, old cloth made all baby dresses, and baby wore nothing else. Baby things were not rinsed out, but scraped off.

Sewing classes for mothers inaugurated a new day for babies. Soft garments were cut and sewed from new yard goods, and babies became more comfortable. Green leaves that seem to grow for no other purpose in the jungle were used for disposable materials, so wash day did not become too much of a problem. Pliable plant leaves up to sizes large enough to afford an umbrella and completely shelter the head and shoulders from a sudden rain, are found there in abundance. They also serve as sheets and blankets in the tiny vine-woven hammocks the women make for their babies.

On a visit to Comiwanda in quest of some women with whom I wanted to talk, I saw an interesting picture. The mother lay on her side nursing one of her twin baby girls. She had her back to the campfire over which she was cooking a monkey whole, and had simply projected a stick through the animal and was roasting it head, arms, tail, and all. The poor monkey looked like nothing so much as a little old man shrivelling with age. I decided not to remain for lunch. The other twin baby was in a tiny vine hammock which swung between two branches of the tree of the palm leaves that formed Comiwanda's shelter. This ingenious mother had fastened one end of a thin pliable vine to the edge of the hammock, and the other to her big toe. And while she nursed one baby, she rocked her foot back and forth on its heel to keep the hammock in motion, and rock-a-bye the other child to sleep. "Just because she is a woman," I thought, "she knows how to care for twins without ever having read a book on child nurture."

To us Miguel's friendship was priceless. Indians who would otherwise have resented our presence accepted us because Miguel did. He was our passport anywhere we wanted to go, and almost always he went with us. He had taken us on as though we were his personal and special project. When our small son was able to stand sturdily on his legs, Miguel's son, a little older, was taught the art of using a bow and arrow which had been made to his specifications. So a miniature bow and arrow had to be made for David, and Miguel instructed him along with his own child.

While Miguel was our best friend, he was also our worst heartache. We had so hoped that he would break with the tribal customs and be one with us at the rising of each full moon, but it seemed that all we had been able to accomplish during the whole month was destroyed in a single night. Men and women who for weeks had conducted themselves with admirable improvement became like things possessed. When once the beating of the tom-tom started, it never ceased until the last number of the group had become too drunk to handle the bones and beat out further tones. Early in the first evening of the festivities there would be a laughter and friendly gaiety which seemed to portend merely light frivolity and amusement, but these soon turned into shrieks and moans as the Indians gave themselves to the passions of wild life and became incensed in drunkenness. *Masato* accomplishes in the red man what whisky and marijuana do in the white. In the madness of burned-incense perfume wives were traded, abducted, given away, or shot full of arrows. Little children were tortured to death merely to make sport for the eyes of voluptuous adults.

We never knew what awfulness our eyes might have to look upon before these times of revelry were over. The debaucheries were always staged back in the interior at Miguel's camp, and once ended were never referred to again. The women of the camp simply began fermenting *masato* in anticipation of the rising of the next full moon, by which time the great trough would again be full, and drunkenness would once more be the order of the day.

Throughout the month this strong man with his wisdom of the forest, knowledge of the ways of the stars, hearty laugh and helping hands, proved his usefulness and faithfulness to us under many circumstances. Repeatedly he dealt with vicious newcomers, and set boundaries beyond which adventurous Indians dared not go.

For eighteen, nineteen, twenty-one months, Miguel lived like a brother with us, but always when the silver moon called, he rushed off into the forest to beat his tom-tom, thus telegraphing an invitation to red men far and wide to come and drink *masato* at his trough in celebration of the rising moon. And how they came! From up river and down. From branch rivers and across the trails. From the depths of the forest. All would drink Miguel's *masato* and make merry. These were nights when we did not talk much—when our nerves were tight and our hearts sick.

Friendships, schooling, industry, new clothing, even haircuts would never change this. This was the outburst of a depraved nature. From birth the elaborate practices of savage ritual had stamped their imprint into the fibers of the boy's developing powers, until as a man he was an epitome of the evil magic of the tribe's ceremonial extravagances.

Between the full-moon festivals Miguel was never drunk. Always he was the popular, handsome leader of men, one who feared nothing but the darkness of night and death. These were synonymous. Nothing had ever hurt him.

Night's darkness was the abode of the spirits of all men

who had ever died. Disembodiment rendered a soul hauntingly powerful and totally demonic. It was the fate of all who die, the loved child, the alluring maiden, the brave hunter, the brutal killer. This was the unquestioned belief of Miguel and all his tribe. Eternity was there in the forest; night extended to forever when a man died. Miguel believed that, and he feared both darkness and death.

One Sunday morning we went to the palm chapel to conduct morning worship. Only a handful of Indians came. Since the previous Friday night they had been drinking and celebrating at Miguel's camp, and they were too drunk this morning to make their way to service. It seemed like a good morning to call it all off—to say we had done all we could—to report home. But the Board in New York could not have understood. Without being there to know the thickness of the shroud that enveloped the souls of men dead in trespasses and sins, it would be impossible to picture the invisible force that gripped the Campas under the spell of the full moon.

Women, whose dainty hands had stroked the soft materials that delighted their merry hearts, and whose ready fingers had learned to use my needles to make nice things for their darling babies, were now back there at Miguel's fire, drunk and debauched and snarling like jungle cats, with eyes flashing hate for everything living.

I had selected my key woman whom I secretly called my aristocrat. She was a little taller than the other women, and a bit straighter. With stately carriage she swept along the jungle path, with never a tilt to the earthen jar of water on her proud head. Many times I had talked to my husband of my hopes for her. If I could win her to faith in the God who had made her and paid the price of her redemption, I could win all the women.

What a rude awakening I had when my stately Bellalopa half swayed and half stumbled into the chapel. My soul sickened at her appearance. Catching the look of disappointment in my eyes, my husband responded with his that he was sorry. Just to know that he cared because I was bent beneath the blow made it easier to pull up a little, and proceed with my part of the service.

But though I sang and quoted Scripture verses for the few Indians present to repeat, I was kneeling at my own altar before God in a petition that had to be granted. For I felt myself hating Bellalopa for being drunk, for having her lovely black hair matted with mud and grass and her brilliant eyes sullied by the tarnish of lewd conduct. It was not for her I was praying, nor for the other women like her, but for myself—that the shutter which was fast closing between my heart and Bellalopa would not lock. If it did, I knew I would never care to touch her again, to plead with her, to help her. God answered my prayer, and I saw the day when Bellalopa became my aristocrat indeed—a royal daughter of the Invisible God. She was made a new creation, and a beautiful and useful life became hers. But all that was much later.

Now in that palm chapel something absolutely unprecedented transpired. My husband, as though he had received an unwritten order from his Commander-in-chief, left the service and walked with quick determined stride over the path to Miguel's stronghold. I felt I must call him back, but I never called my husband back when he walked like that. I knew he was going to confront Miguel in his ugly drunkenness. Miguel had been careful never to let the white man see him drunk, Miguel who was our best friend and worst enemy. He would hate the white man for coming to him now. I began to sketch plans, should I be left alone in the jungle that night.

Maybe an hour later, maybe two hours, my husband returned to the bungalow. Miguel had been sullen, subtle and talkative. He had suggested that the only reason the white man had for being there was because he and his tribe were as they were. He was really doing the white man a favor by getting himself into that condition, for it created employment for the man from the far land. The spirit of evil was having a last vicious fling in Miguel, as he whipped this red man's mind into a tempest of sneering suggestions—all meant to dishearten the man who would willingly have given his life for Miguel and his people—who later actually did just that.

On Monday noon Miguel approached the bungalow and asked to see the white man. The two men greeted each other, and then sat on the veranda without a word passing between them. Finally the visitor arose, hesitated for a moment, and then walked slowly back into the forest. The next day at high noon he came again to talk to the white man, but again silence stood like a third party between them.

Through the screened enclosure that separated my dining room from the veranda I watched the two silent figures, and it seemed to me I must start conversation for them. There was so much that could be said, but it was not my interview. The white man was waiting for the red man to talk. It was the red man who had come, and what was in his heart the white man dared not suggest. Of one thing the white man was sure; deep conviction had settled upon the heart of the leader of the Campas. If conviction was there, it had been put there by the Spirit of God, and that same Spirit would have to undertake the work if spiritual birth was to come.

Like the vigilant tarrying of the physician, the white man allowed time for a good birth. But eventually the convicted Miguel began to express himself. He reasoned that as long as he held his *masato* parties for the tribe, the work of the white man would not prosper. The white man gave assent to that. Then Miguel suggested that it might be well for him to call all his friends back to his camp and tell them he was through with the old ways, that he was accepting the white man's God and the white man's teaching. Following such a dramatic announcement, the physician with the skilled fingers of love helped to bring to birth the soul of the red man. With determination and purpose in his black eyes, Miguel asked the white man to go with him to his fire. There he beat his tom-tom to signal his call to the tribe, some of whom had not yet reached their own camps but were slowly poling their way up stream or lazily floating down river. Others were crossing the trails into the interior. When they heard the tom-tom message they naturally questioned its purpose. Miguel would not have another trough of *masato* yet, for they had just emptied it! It would take until another full moon to process enough more to offer to his friends. Nevertheless, they had such confidence in Miguel that when he called they came without undue delay.

All afternoon, all evening, into the small hours of the night, they came. When it was very late and most of them had arrived, Miguel turned upside down the empty trough which he had made from the trunk of a cedar tree. Two forked sticks held it up from the ground, and beneath it he built a raging fire from end to end, which soon turned it to charcoal before the fear-filled eyes of his tribesmen. At such sacrilege they actually trembled. Quickly he explained that this was his method of demonstrating that he was through with all the vicious ceremonial ways of the tribe, that since he now possessed a new heart, his ways must be new also.

Heaven bent low over the jungle that night. Centuries before, according to the Scriptures, God had said to His servant and friend, "Get thee out of thy country, and from thy kindred, away from thy father's house, unto a land that I will show thee: and I will make of thee a great nation. . . . In blessing I will bless thee, and in multiplying I will multiply thy seed as the stars of the heaven, and as the sand which is upon the sea shore."

We had witnessed the first conversion among the Campa Indians, and it seemed a pledge that many from this sand-born tribe of earth should come to know spiritual birth, and be among the hosts of those who shine as stars in the firmament. This has indeed come true.

FLAME FLOWERS

A POISED beauty stood in her canoe, gazing at her reflection in the crystal clear river as with a stem of the palm leaf she etched a red design in fine lines of intricate pattern over her face. The brilliant coral wings of a parrot were in her hair, and strands of red beans crisscrossed her shoulders. The blossoming flame vines which spread like shafts of sunset over the trees at the forest's edge where the river breaks its fastness were no more colorful than this woman of the forest.

Jungle women are both repulsive and enticing and I have censured and envied them on occasion. Their laughter is quick, ascending the scale to end on a ringing high C that resounds through the woods. The reason for their gaiety is not always apparent; it seems to be an expression of a way of being rather than the result of any cause.

As elsewhere, so in the jungle, some of the girls are pretty and the women beautiful. The tiniest girl dresses exactly like her mother, except that the nut shells and bones which adorn her garment are miniatures to match her own tiny self.

The hair of every girl and woman is arranged in identical

fashion, in heavy bangs hanging as it grows, sometimes to the shoulders, sometimes to the waist. It is never braided or fastened up. That moving, gleaming object is perhaps an iridescent winged beetle with clutching claws which she has placed in her hair as an ornament.

A tiny monkey smaller than your hand may be clinging to her garment, or nestling on her head. Monkeys are chattering creatures which afford much fun with their mischievous ways. A person soon learns in the jungle not to pet monkeys unless he wants them as a permanent possession. You cannot pet them and leave them. Once you have petted them they belong to you, and they will cling to you with all four legs and a tail. Separation is next to impossible. Feed one small bit of banana to a monkey and he is yours for life.

Not only were there tiny monkeys, but monkeys of every size. Day monkeys and night monkeys. The big-eyed nocturnals took possession of our place at night, scampering over the roof and hanging from the eaves, begging attention. Monkeys ranged from the pocket-piece size to the great night howling coto, which was as large as a good-sized boy and just as noisy.

Monkeys and parrots were pets at every campfire, and joined with the chattering and screeching of birds and beasts and the laughing of women to make the forest reverberate with gaiety at times of special merriment. It was the sound of a free life in the open without inhibitions. I liked it.

Life at a campfire is enjoyed by the North American woman on vacation, but it is not her idea of a daily routine. Bamboo walls are good at first but soon dry out and leave spaces as wide as the bamboo itself. I hung lengths of material for curtains to create a bit of privacy, but my Indian neighbors seemed to feel no need of any shelter. They had never had it.

When we finally moved into our cedar bungalow, I had

rooms with screened windows and doors, but the forest women still lived at their open fires, not envying me at all. They would not want to be bothered with my utensils of civilization. When house-cleaning time came for me I had to dust, wash, clean, and polish, while the Indian women just broke pieces from a burning log, set fire to the little leaf hut, and burned it down, dirt and all. Then a few rods away they erected fresh branches for shade, and that was a new house. Spring cleaning time made me do some serious thinking, for they seemed to have a better system than mine.

After meals they also had the advantage of me. While I slavishly washed china, polished silver, rinsed tea towels, and ironed linens, they merely arose from the campfire; the meal was not only ended but there were no restorations to order, no cooking utensils to be put away. The earthen vessels which hold their water cannot be subjected to fire. They use gourds, but not for cooking. So there are no dishes or pots and pans to wash. This I would have liked.

When I arrived in the jungle there was no place to put my few belongings if I unpacked them, so except for such as we used daily, they stayed in their boxes until our house was built. When I discovered that the Indian women had absolutely nothing, I was almost afraid to display my possessions for fear of making them envious and discontented. But I could have spared my fears; they simply did not want the kind of things which to me constituted the essentials of life.

Life was simplicity itself among the natives. The women told me quite frankly that they had their babies because they wanted them. The secrets of planned parenthood were not unknown to them; there was a tea they could make from the bark of a tree which would serve their purpose. But they would not use it; they wanted their babies. Yet, though many babies were born, a large family was practically unknown, for more little ones died than lived. When I came to realize the absolute lack of assistance in delivery, the unsanitary conditions under which children came into the world, and their exposure, I was amazed that any of them lived.

No one stays around when a child is to be born, for everyone is afraid the mother will die, and to see her die brings a haunting experience into a life. With heartless fatalism they reason that if she is to die she will die. There is nothing they can do to prevent it. So they go away and give her plenty of time. The husband, his other wives, and all the children leave the mother and return much later. If she is alive, well and good, but if she is dead they did not see her die. That is heathenism. That is just the absence of Christianity.

Jungle women are something special. Because they are women, they manage when there is seemingly no way to manage. The Campa woman delivers her own baby into the soft, warm ashes at her campfire. No better receiving blanket could be found in the jungle. She uses a piece of burning charcoal picked up from the fire as her surgical shears. Fire is the antiseptic implement of safety for herself and baby.

To observe an Indian woman care for her infant is a revelation of an intuition native to her sex, altogether apart from civilization. I had considered my little white enamel baby tub an absolute necessity, and I was endlessly glad I had taken it along, but the Indian mother bathed her baby without a tub. I watched the Indian baby's bathing with a bit of shock, with a controlled desire to laugh, yet with a nod of admiration to one who managed without book of instruction or mechanical equipment. The dark-skinned mother stooped to the river's edge and filled her mouth with water, held it until her tongue told her it was the right temperature for baby's bath, then holding her infant in mid-air, administered a fine spray from between her white teeth, showering the child up and down the front. Then she turned him and completed the shower on his back. For a Turkish towel she used the palms of her hands; she let the sun do the rest. Not bad! My book had told me to test the temperature of baby's bath with my elbow. The jungle woman had no book, but she got the temperature right just the same.

The jungle baby's feeding time is whenever he wants to nurse, for he finds a full breast always conveniently at hand above the top of the mother's garment. When her hands are occupied with the spinning of cotton thread, a walking tot will stand beside her in most picturesque fashion and help himself. Such infancy and childhood produce sturdy men who become great hunters. I found it difficult to win my arguments for a slightly different procedure among the women; the success of their time-honored custom caused them to inquire, "Why?"

No mother knows how old her baby is after the fourth moon has passed over his head, for their numerical system allows counting only to four. After that it is another and another, but no more numbers. They really need no more figures. They have no money to count, and years are not important, as no one ever gets old. There is much sickness and no remedies. There is constant warfare with other tribes. So death is the order of the day, and they just have no old folks.

When babies are less than a month old, they are fed the root of the yuca tree, which is exceedingly starchy. In Brazil it is called *manioc*; in the inland it is *casava*. It is the root from which tapioca is made. A branch is broken from the tree at a joint and pushed into the moist jungle soil. The natural jungle growth must be pulled away from it until eight months have passed, then the roots are ready to be eaten. You never harvest a crop of yuca. It becomes dark on the second day after it is dug, so you just dig enough for one day. The best roots are three to four inches in diameter and three to four feet in length, and are covered with a thick brown bark. When this bark is removed the root is white, slippery and brittle. While holding the peeled root you strike into it with a heavy knife, and snap it off into pieces for cooking.

The Indian does not peel his yuca but pushes it under the coals of his fire and bakes it. There is no better way of preparing it, but for variety I peeled it and boiled it in water. For lunch, since I had boiled it for breakfast, I cut the pieces and browned them over the fire. Then for a change at dinner, I ground the cold, cooked root and made a patty, pressing a bit of wild meat into the center. When I was fortunate enough to have a supply of lard I sliced the raw roots and fried them like potato chips. They were much harder than potatoes, but were very good, and this additional way of preparation added interest.

For a person to say that he was tired of yuca root was to place himself under indictment, and it became a rule of the house that the chief entrée was not to be discussed. Everyone was tired of it. No one liked it, and that particularly because there was nothing to like about it. It was almost tasteless. It tasted like tapioca would taste unless you put something in it to make it taste like what you put in. You had to eat yuca root for it was all you had, and you would continue eating it for that is what you would continue to have. So you did not talk about it.

The weather was another subject that was taboo, at least so far as the heat was concerned. You just did not say, "How desperately hot it is!" Of course it was hot, and it was going to become hotter, but every one else was just as uncomfortable as yourself. So you just did not talk about it. It was far easier to endure the heat and to eat yuca root three times every day when you did not complain about them. The more you felt you had to mention them, the more you exercised conversational ingenuity to supply substitutes for the forbidden subjects. It was a valuable course of study, lacking only a professor to preside over the class.

To feed a three-month-old infant yuca root was obviously out of all reason, and I knew that I must protest to the mothers about it. For if I cut a bowl full of the root in pieces, and covered it with water overnight, I had two inches of starch. To see a forest mother feed that root to her baby was almost too much for my inner decision never to be surprised at anything they did. But I decided to postpone my instruction since they were breaking so many essential rules for the continuance of life in a wooded world. Yet when I saw a woman fill her mouth with a quantity of yuca root, chew it well, then blow it down her infant's throat, I left the scene in haste. Of course the child eventually learned to swallow, but until he did, that was her method of forced feeding.

Miguelina was older than the mothers of the tiny babies, and was more mature in judgment. I told her to urge the young mothers not to feed their babies yuca root in that fashion. But she merely shrugged her shoulders, saying that they had all raised their children that way. Since she had two sons with marvelous bodies there was little I could say in rebuttal. After all, I consoled myself, lacking the bottles of predigested baby foods of drug stores, the women were obtaining the same results.

The jungle furnishes so few alternatives. You must accept one way because of the total absence of any other way. When a mother dies the baby will die also, for there is no substitute for mother's milk. They have no domestic animals and no commercially prepared foods. Just jungle.

There are times when another nursing mother could give nourishment to an orphan baby, but the woman would have to be the wife of a man who is not an enemy of the baby's father. And there is so much enmity among the Indians that this rule generally bars the woman who could save the baby's life. The father prefers to toss his baby into the river to follow

the body of its mother than to hear it cry for three days in
starvation and then die anyway.

To become righteously indignant over such practices is
one thing, and to change them is another. It was our problem
to do something for the babies, yet satisfy the fathers. We had
no milk, except the costly tins of dried milk we had taken
for our own baby. We attempted to use evaporated milk, but
nine tins out of twelve bulged and three of them exploded, so
evaporated milk was not the answer. Powdered milk was expensive and we could not supply the jungle folks with that.
So cows would have to be imported.

While a slender, sure-footed mule could pick his way
over the mountain trail, clumsy cows would never make it.
These would have to be brought from the east in flat-bot-
tomed dugouts along the river. In time, five head of Brown
Swiss cattle were brought. Then began the fight to keep them
alive. Leopards sought them every night, so it was necessary
to corral them at sundown. Fires were kept burning in the
little clearing to discourage the prowling of the great cats near
our camp. Even during the daytime, the cattle had to be
fenced to prevent straying into the cool green forest from
which they would not have returned. Hungry leopards are
on the hunt even by day.

There was nothing to feed the cattle except jungle grass.
To have that it was necessary to clear out the large trees and
smaller growth so that the sun could reach the soil and encourage the regrowth of the jungle. When a tree is cut out,
six small ones spring up to take its place, and when a shrub is
removed a small forest of shrubs leaps up. You never conquer
a jungle. You just keep fighting it.

The milk was very thin but we had plenty of it. As soon
as it was drawn I boiled it. We were not prepared then to
test the herd, so it was safest to protect ourselves by boiling
the milk. When it cooled, I skimmed off the bit of cream

which rose to the top, and pressed it through a sieve so as to get a small pitcher of it. Cream was a luxury, and it must be used to best advantage.

The Indians would use neither milk nor veal. They had superstitions about deer, and thought veal too much like them to be suitable for food. Eventually the pasture land was enlarged, grass became more plentiful, and a better species was planted. The herd increased and the milk became richer. Pounds of butter were made. This all took time, a persistent and continuous struggle against odds.

The natives finally decided that milk and veal could be risked, just as they eventually learned that the white people could be trusted. Residence near us effected many changes in their ways of thinking and doing. Our remedies cured their sicknesses. Our counsel improved their ways. Now their babies were cared for by our provisions, and many ghastly things which had long been their established custom were discontinued. They tried to make us forget they had ever done them. We honestly tried to forget.

WILDERNESS CONQUESTS

THE PIONEER does not mistake poverty for piety. He knows to live at all he must live the best he can. Life can be lived in the open in the tropics, but the white man builds houses and makes homes and teaches others to do likewise.

Though we were eight hundred feet above sea level, it was hot. Instead of summer and winter we had wet and dry seasons, the difference being that in the dry season it rained, and in the wet season it poured.

While the rain was falling, we thought the air certainly would become a bit cooler, but when it stopped steam rose from the ground and vegetation and it seemed to be hotter than ever. Our lives were saved by the coolness of the late night. Even a light woolen blanket was required on occasion.

While bamboo-palm houses thatched with palm leaves look inviting in a travel book, they certainly are not substantial. They are infested with all types of creeping and crawling things. Lizards of varying hues and sizes dart among the palms and peer out by day and night. Scaly fat-legged things do not induce sleep and restfulness, and there were hordes of them.

Parakeets are lovely birds. One in a cage can be both entertaining and charming, but flocks of them on your roof and floor, following you about, repeating what you say, can become intolerable. Any one of the little birds, if permitted to sit on my shoulder would pour affection into my ear. If taken on my finger she would turn her pretty head, look me directly in the eye, and assure me that she and her chattering companions were one hundred per cent for me with all their lovely finery. But put down, she would join the group, nudge them with her head, sway against them with her body, and set the whole flock to exchanging small talk with such mirthful amusement that they would literally bend their heads to the ground and nearly keel over with laughter. I wondered what they really said.

Yellowhead parrots were the best talkers. They joined their screeching calls with the coral and green parrots when some cause of excitement started laughter and talking among the Indians at the campfire. The great red and blue, and blue and gold macaws, were as vicious as they were beautiful. All these creatures, whether interesting or repulsive, invaded our palm house. There was no defense against them, no seclusion from them.

Small darting things were of less concern than the snakes. As might be expected, big thick serpents found their way into the palm roofs of our buildings. Once a twelve-foot baby boa constrictor spent the night on the roof over my head. I tried to convince myself that the noise I heard might be one of the big parrots, but I knew it was not. For another hour I argued that it could be a little monkey; that also I knew it was not. Next morning proved that it was just what I had thought it was—a snake seeking a resting place. A pole was lifted to the roof, the snake wound itself around it, and was taken away and killed. How I loathed it! I detested every snake in the jungle, even the coral snake that flashes its diamonds of jet and flame in jewel-like pattern. I hated them all. I do not even like women who do not hate snakes.

Fully as alarming as the creeping things were the columns of fog which drifted into my sleeping place and stood bending over my hammock when I opened my eyes in the early dawn. They were like ghostly figures beckoning me to get up and go with them. Every night and morning I longed for the completion of the cedar bungalow we planned to build. When once inside cedar walls with a screened door to hook, I knew I would be protected from many of the things that now troubled me most. I would be glad to cease fire against at least a few of my enemies.

To build a house in a jungle takes time. The nearest sawmill was a thousand miles downstream on the big river. Large launches could come only halfway, and the last five hundred miles must be done in small craft. Sawed cedar was ordered and eventually arrived. We built a cedar bungalow, nothing to boast about particularly as it was not much more modern than the palm building we had been using, but at least it was solid.

In gay moments I told myself that my palm building was quite up-to-date. I had running water and a sink. By that I meant that I went running down to the river's bank and brought water in pails; then when finished with it, I would pour it on the floor and it would leak through. The floors were of split bamboo. The rounded sides turned up and you had to walk on them as a midget would walk on corrugated cardboard. It was necessary to sweep them lengthwise. But openwork floors had their points, for crumbs of any foods were immediately carried away by ants which eagerly anticipated their fall, while vultures with naked heads and greedy appetites circled over any decayed matter, settled like great black umbrellas on the corpse, then lumbered away leaving only a skeleton behind.

Filth is not a problem in the jungle, for the frequent torrents of rain convey waste into the porous forest earth. The stench which is so prevalent in the coastal and mountain cities, even within a block of the main street, is totally absent from the jungle.

A young German, who merely identified himself as Franz, had run away from home when he was twelve years old and had remained on the west coast of South America. When Franz heard that his father, the captain on a steamer, was coming into port at Callao, he feared that he might be discovered and taken to task for the nine years of anguish he had caused, and so fled into the jungle.

A palm bridge gave way under him, and a piece of palm pierced the calloused bottom of his foot and snapped off. By the time he reached our place, his leg was badly swollen and he was in a serious condition from infection. I drew the foreign matter out of his foot with a poultice of brown soap and *chancaca*, a hard brown native sugar, and he rapidly improved. He appeared to like my nursing and cooking; certainly he liked assisting my husband. At first he remained with us because he could not walk, then because he desired to be there. He helped dig two cisterns which were lined with material almost as costly as gold dust, for cement had to be imported from the outside world.

One night, troubled in sleep, Franz brushed at his pillow, while turning over a number of times in drowsiness. Finally he became awake, and struck a match to see what was touching his head and face. There on his pillow he found a snake making himself at home. He quickly slashed it with his knife, for without a knife a person never lies down to sleep in the jungle. In the morning a big Indian turned pale-face when he looked at the reptile, for he recognized it as one of the most deadly snakes the Indians know. Is it any wonder that the

German always quaked whenever the snake was mentioned afterward?

There were many reasons why I was anxious to have the building rushed. For one, there was no room into which the Indians did not come, no cooking kettle into which they did not peek. Like the tots that climbed into the old man's turret of Longfellow's "Children's Hour," they seemed to be everywhere. The Indians had no privacy in their own lives, and they saw no reason why anyone else should want it. But I did. The little privacy I enjoyed was provided not by walls and closed doors, but by sheer authority of my husband's word, the deep growl of our German police dog, Laddie, and the mesh folds of a mosquito tent.

In a palm house there are no clothes closets. Garments not in service are kept in metal boxes, but corrosion caused by a cake of soap, a tube of toothpaste, a flashlight battery, a piece of moist leather, or one of many things may destroy all the contents of a packing case. A suit or dress if hung on a peg is searched diligently by self-appointed cleaners, the cockroaches, which, if they discover any food stain, remove not only the spot but the material. They ate the paint off my bucket and panhandles, and the color and lettering off my books, leaving as the binding only cheesecloth over cardboard. Betty Crocker's red and blue cookbook turned a sickly white at their hands.

I could not use many of the recipes anyway, for it was necessary to substitute about five ingredients in every recipe and omit three others, so it was easier to improvise my own. To put tempting and varied preparations on the table required real ingenuity, for there was almost nothing from which to make them.

Whatever the Indians ate we had to learn to eat. We did not need to eat them their way, nor prepare them their way, although I must confess their way was generally best. The yuca root, if left in its bark and buried under the coals of the campfire, was more tasty than when prepared in any other manner. It did not taste like baked potato, though we used it as a potato substitute because of its high starch content.

Green bananas fried in fat were exceptionally good, and we always served them with fish. But fat was not often to be had—only when the good captain of the mail launch found some down river, and brought it to us in five-gallon gasoline tins soldered shut. It was liquid, as was the butter we occasionally got from Argentina, so we spooned it instead of trying to spread it with a knife. This contributed toward a balanced budget, for less of it is used when it is more like oil than butter. It seems to suffer from loss of personality.

But fried ripe plantains! They are really good! Plantains are the vegetable banana, coarse, large, and eaten raw by the Indians. Cut lengthwise and fried or baked with a bit of native brown sugar, they are delicious. We ate them every day.

Wild game was not easy to accept. To me game was something we were forced to eat at home in childhood when one of my uncles returned from a hunt in Canada. But here in the woods there was nothing but wild meat, so we learned to like it. At first I drowned it in sour juice squeezed from a lime-lemon fruit which grew in the region. This fresh juice replaced the wild taste of the game with a citrus flavor. After a struggle I decided to accept the meat for what it was, and before leaving jungle life I could honestly enjoy my smothered *liebre*, roast loin of *huangana*, baked *sacha-vaca*, and other such dainties which appeared regularly on my dinner menus. All were really very good now.

It was rather trying to have to get along without bread, but there was neither grain nor cereal. Flour could not be brought to us over the trail unless packed in soldered tin containers. That was too expensive. The cargo mules swim the rivers, and whatever they carry is subject to submersion. Wet flour cannot be redeemed. This item would have to come from the east, and flour from Argentina would be as expensive and not as good as flour from the United States. So we ordered flour from New York, flour which finished its seven-thousand mile trip to us by water in open dugouts. Sometimes it was green with mold when it arrived. Such spoilage made the few bags that did reach us in good condition exceedingly expensive, and there was very little money in the flour budget. Bread therefore was high on the luxury list.

During the two years we lived in Ecuador we used the kind of yeast that is kept in a glass jar between bakings. When a jar of yeast exploded, an urgent SOS reached us from a neighboring mission station which we gladly supplied though it left us without any. That was on the coast, but in the interior there are no neighboring stations, and that kind of yeast does not belong to the jungle.

We ordered Magic Yeast from Chicago, and soon a small tin box began to bring five yeast cakes in every first class mail. When yeast arrived from the west coincidentally with flour from the east I made bread. You can never know how good bread can smell and taste until you have had none for months, and then bake it.

Suddenly my yeast stopped coming. The suppliers wrote that they had made shipment on the designated dates, but it did not arrive. Then Perez, a muleteer, visited us. When I mentioned my failure to receive the yeast, he said he knew the reason. Government mail is carried over the trail, and the keeper of the little post at the end of each day's travel is a government employee who handles it. The curiosity of one of these men became so much aroused by the tiny package addressed to the American lady that he opened one to discover the contents. Inside he found a tablet, which when added to his home brew, injected quite a kick. After that I received my yeast only once in a long, long time!

You would think we would have done something about it! That we would have insisted that our yeast be delivered, since we knew what was happening to it! We did do something about it, but we got exactly as much yeast as if we had done nothing. Things look quite different to government officials along a mule trail so far from headquarters as to involve a long arduous journey. They wonder what we crazy missionaries are doing out there, anyway.

The yeast problem was partially solved by my Spanish maid, Alcinda. For seven months I had been without any help. There was no use trying to get a girl to come from the coast; that was out. Since we had friends on the Amazon river where it begins a thousand miles east of us, we asked them to please find a girl who would come up the river and work for us. A slim Spanish girl, with a bitter outlook on society in general, was the answer. She decided that life with us would be a daring novelty, so took the first possible river boat before she had time to change her mind. She proved to be a gem—proud, capable, adventurous. She adored my baby, admired my husband, loved me. At the end of the first year our cup of joy overflowed when she accepted our faith, and as a Christian sparkled with an inner light.

It was this Alcinda who knew what to do about yeast. She leavened a mixture of cornmeal with our two remaining yeast cakes, then cut homemade cakes from the rolled-out dough. These little golden squares she placed on muslin in the sun, and turned them every few minutes, never permitting the sun to leave them. It had to be a day when the sun promised to shine continuously with not so much as one cloud interfering. When the cakes were thoroughly dried, she put them in a muslin bag and hung them in a dry place. They were almost as good as commercial yeast.

We found an Indian with some corn, and discovered that up one of the branch rivers they grew a little of it. When we planted it we found that it grew marvelously. Came the night when on the morrow we planned to enjoy some of the golden corn. But that proved to be the night a drove of water hogs had selected to snort their way over the river's bank in search of food. They devoured our entire crop!

Like the Pilgrims, we planted corn again, and this time when it was ready either for wild hogs or us, we coaxed the Indians to make campfires in the corn field to keep the water hogs from coming ashore. They were willing, but of course many of them were required to do it. They brought their families with them, and while keeping the fires ablaze throughout the night, roasted and ate nearly as much fresh corn as the wild hogs had devoured on the previous occasion.

Then we planted corn again—this time enough both for the Indians and ourselves. We found that we could grow three crops each year. From that time on our menu took on many new items—corn muffins, popovers, johnnycake, dressing for fish, and stuffing for wild birds. Corn was certainly a welcome addition to our diet.

A little grist mill had come with us, and now was like a friend. The man who had taken me to the jungle had seemed to foresee every possible contingency. Equipment which seemed utterly without purpose at the time was taken in anticipation of later need. And I constantly marveled at the things Ross knew how to do. Among other things he had included books of information on how to make things—charcoal, for instance.

It was with as much pride as if we were the original inventors of charcoal that we stood waiting that first time for the steam to rise when the smoke signal through the little chimney-opening was just right, and water had been poured on the hot clay mound which covered the wood. When we broke the clay, we saw the charcoal gleaming in readiness to produce the hottest fire possible for the little forge in the carpenter shop, for kettles in the kitchen, and for the iron Alcinda had brought with her from the city on the big river. We had made charcoal! We had never done it before, had never known how to. But the little book had told us. Now we could try something else.

Did you ever press with a charcoal iron? I had seen such contrivances on the sidewalks of Lima. At the time a tailor was making expensive suits for men. He sat on the floor of his shop, and operated a sewing machine by turning a wheel with his hand. The iron he used was one of these charcoal creations, which when not needed he set on the stones of the sidewalk outside his door.

This type of iron has a charcoal compartment at the bottom, where a small door permits the fuel to be placed inside. It is lighted, and as the iron is used, the movement fans the coals into a very hot fire. Alcinda could do as beautiful work with one as any I have ever seen.

I had brought with me a gasoline iron with a tiny ball that holds the inflammable fluid, but Alcinda was afraid to use it. It sputtered, and the very thought of gasoline terrified her. So after her first attempt I never asked her to use it again. It was not necessary, for her iron was just as good.

We did not wait for our house to be completed before we moved into it. Indeed we occupied the first corner in which a floor was laid, and proceeded to build the rest of the structure around us. That was not the right way, but the best way.

I thought the millennium would come before the house was finished. The Indians were not much help, and the lumber when it arrived from the distant sawmill still had to be planed. I helped some with that. But beyond that simple work I am afraid that I was not much of a carpenter. That was not my calling, and I had neither the knowledge, time nor strength for it—and I might as well add—the desire.

Ross had his hands full, building a house for himself, while at the same time trying to teach red men to make plantations in clearing the white man's way. Certainly the wilderness would never have been vanquished had he let the natives do it their way; one half-acre would have been thoroughly reforested before the next half-acre had been cut down. While building and clearing, Ross was also learning two tribal languages and doctoring the sick folks of both tribes. We would just have to get someone to come to our aid.

A young man in North America, Thomas Willey, responded to the call to do some carpentry work as his part in carrying out the Great Commission, and came out to help. How glad we were to see him. Hardly had he got settled before he informed us that one of the things he had checked on the list of items he would never do during his whole lifetime was marry. We wondered why, for he was big, handsome, talented and vivacious, a delightful addition to the household. More important still, he was a lover of tools and lumber, and grew eloquent over the fragrant cedar of our house. He stroked the ebony pillars on which it rested as if they were rare museum pieces.

Forest life was fascinating to the newcomer. He was happy and a good helper, but after a few months he returned to North America. Then, contrary to all his misogamist vows, Thomas married a lovely girl, and whisked her off with him to another mission field. He said that living with us in the jungle did something to him. In any case, our field lost a good man, but another field gained a good couple.

Now we were really up against it, for we needed a carpenter badly. One day we heard about a young German by the name of Antonio Christoff who had come from a monastery in Berlin into the jungle east of us, as an aid to an older man who had been in the region for years. But upon arrival Tony, as he preferred to be called, would not accept the work. Nor could he return to Berlin as only his one-way passage had been paid. The report was that he was a skillful woodworker.

We sent a runner posthaste to see if we could secure him; by working for us he could earn his passage home. So anxious was he that he did not even wait to answer our note, but returned with our runner. We called him Tony, and he was a godsend to us, yet the most mysterious and difficult person to deal with we ever encountered. More than once we wondered whether he had been sent to help us or torment us. When at times we thought we had solved the puzzle of his personality, he would do something to cause the mystery to deepen, and we would find ourselves right back where we started. One day he was smart and sweet, and the next muddling and bitter.

At breakfast Tony and my husband would lay out their plans in detail for the day in the best man-to-man, friend-to-friend tradition. He would smile at me across the table and praise my food and housekeeping with genuine Continental courtesy. Then, in less than an hour, as though an evil fire had flared in his brain, he would destroy valuable lumber and tools, and curse the world and all its inhabitants. At such times my heart would curl up in its fortress-from-fear corner, and simply wait. But my husband, as if he had drawn the phlegmatism from the Indians, continued with his work as though nothing had happened.

Months of this went on. A sweet tenderness would flow from the heart of the man from Berlin when he talked to me of Ross, and that was often. I felt he was not only revealing his admiration for the strong man who never lost his temper, and who never scolded him for losing his, but in an indirect way was apologizing for his own lack of self-control.

The monk was more than a carpenter; he was a skilled cabinet maker, and at one time had specialized in building automobile panel boards. This strange man designed ceilings and floors for our rooms, fitting various shades of cedar into artistic patterns, and tongued, grooved and glued them without use of nails. They were simply beautiful. The walls were ten-inch panels fitted into two-inch strips of off-shade cedar. He polished the whole room with wild beeswax dissolved in kerosene, and eventually my little house was like a rosy, fragrant cedar chest.

Meanwhile he had a secret project under way in his room. Ross knew about it, but I was not allowed to get a glimpse. When the time for the unveiling came, Tony presented me with a beautiful book table on which he had carved grapes in natural size. This was his quiet way of expressing appreciation for little kindnesses. My expression of delight brought tears to the lashes of eyes which I had seen burn with such passion that I had feared for my husband's life, when hatchets, chisels, and wood knives sailed through the air without regard for consequences.

The violin was his first love, and he played it like a master. There was scarcely a night when its strains were not heard. On Sunday there was no carpentry on the mission property, and he attended our services in the open palm chapel, joining heartily in the singing. At family worship he prayed in German, and while we understood but little of the language, we felt he was in earnest.

After seven months Tony confessed a need in his life, a need which we knew if met would make him the kind of man he longed to be. It was a day of rejoicing in the camp when he accepted Christ as Saviour. Soon he learned the strength which comes from full surrender to the Lord, and then the man who had so frequently been whipped into a fury by the sin-ruined nature with which he was physically born, found the satisfaction of the abundant life through a new nature into which he had been spiritually born.

Tony told us that there was a girl in Germany who was the mother of his child. Could he have her come to the Peruvian jungle? Could he marry her and make a home for her with us? He certainly could and did. Edella was a beautiful woman with the loveliest hair I have ever seen. It was black and curly, and she wore it beautifully. Her clothes were not those of the jungle, for she was a talented seamstress, who back home might well have been a fashion model. Yet this woman of Old World culture accepted jungle life quite graciously. She and Tony were married on the coast, and immediately on arrival she made a home for Tony and their son. But life was not easy there, and before she accepted her husband's new faith, she would yield to anger and vile outbursts of temper which rivaled those of Tony in former times. With white-hot rage she would demand things that could not be granted. She would jerk up my precious flower plants by the roots, and actually spit in my husband's face. But he expected to see Edella become a Christian one day, so he simply took it, though steadfastly refusing to yield on the vital principle.

When our bungalow was finished, our work among the Indians had so increased that the Board sent out a second couple to help. Another bungalow was needed, and Tony stayed to build it. He firmly believed that his coming to Peru, with its early disappointment and disillusionment, had been in the divine plan to bring him into a knowledge of salvation and victory. I think that was true.

LURID LORE

Daily the Campas greeted the rising sun with hideous shrieks and screams, a salute to their returning god. Was it not the sun which dispelled their most feared enemy, night? And should he not consequently be accepted as their best friend?

Next to death, the Indian is most afraid of night. He is not afraid of the leopard, for he can kill the leopard with his bow and arrow. He does not fear man, for he has just as good a chance of killing a man as any man has of harming him. But the Campa does fear death, and since night to him is the fore-shadowing of death, he dreads night.

The forest man believes his soul to be immortal, but un-like his North American brother, he has no theory of a happy hunting ground for his eternal habitation. In South America, the Indians believe that at death their disembodied spirits will resume the trek on the jungle trail and walk throughout an endless eternity, seeking a place of abode—that they will visit the campfires of the living every night, hoping to be admitted to live again where there is light and friendliness. Night is the abode of the dead, and every disembodied spirit is an evil spirit, whether it be the spirit of your own child, your bitterest enemy, or your treasured love.

One day an Indian woman I had never seen before came down the river on a balsa raft and hurried to me over the river's bank. In her arms was a dying baby which she pressed into my hands. With an indescribably pathetic plea in her black eyes, and a deep sob in her voice, she begged me not to let her baby die.

Since several of her husband's other wives had been at our post and received physical help, she believed I could make her baby live. I feared that I could not, for already pneumonia was snuffing out the child's life. But for two hours I worked, doing everything possible with the limited equipment at hand. Again and again that mother would take her child and do the things any mother would do for her baby, and then in sobbing despair return it to me with the plea repeated that I make it live.

When I first arrived in this forest-world where the women seemed so different from those I had seen elsewhere, I wondered how I could possibly help them. Their response was so slow, their ways so crude. Many times I questioned my ability to do anything worth while for them. Never had I read about people anywhere in so primitive a way of life as these.

But during those hours of laboring over this child, there came to me an understanding of what these women really were like, and an answer to the question how I could help them. From the expression on that woman's face, the fear in her eyes, the sob in her throat, the plea in the movement of her hands, I learned that she was just a woman—a mother—like any other woman, any other mother I had ever known, except that she had no hope. I knew the way of hope, and I could teach it to her.

In spite of all our efforts, this precious little one slipped away, leaving the mother with no comprehension except that of loss and dread. We prepared the body for burial, wrapping it in clean white muslin, and placing it in an appropriate box. So far as we know this was the first Campa baby ever prepared for burial. These Indians do not bury; they simply toss the body into the river.

When I placed the woman's baby before her, she picked up the filthy dressings and put them directly on top of the child's face with an expression of finality which revealed more plainly than words the thoughts of her heart. It was loss, utter and complete, for the Indians have no knowledge of the resurrection.

The Indian mother believes that when her baby dies she begins a relationship with the tiny disembodied spirit instead of with its bodily presence. When she makes a balsa-log raft to travel on the river, she must also make a tiny raft and tie it behind her own in order to provide transportation for the wee spirit, even though now it is an evil spirit. When she comes to a fallen log she must mark her path with stakes so that the little spirit may follow her. At her campfire she will be molested with the haunting presence of the spirit.

It took us quite a while to teach the Indians about the place of confinement for disembodied evil spirits, and of a heaven of light and delight for the spirits of babies and Christian adults. But this was a part of our glorious message— truths which delivered them from the bondage of darkness and the chains of captivity. Theirs was the dark prison of ignorance. It was an indescribable delight for us to sit by the campfire in the evening hours and teach truths that set a glow in the eyes of the forest people which outshone the luminous embers.

Campfires are the very life of the jungle, the center both of daytime and night affairs. Eating and visiting take place at

the fires, for they afford protection from vampire bats, leopards, and other molesters. But the fire means much more than
that. For when the sun sets the Campa's god is gone, so they
rekindle campfires to provide the light that becomes a man-
made god for the hours of darkness. The shadows beyond the
fire are the abode of evil spirits, so Indians stay within the
light of their fires until night is gone. This practice provided
a splendid foundation for teaching about the true God, who
having made the sun and man, also provided an abode for
man's spirit for time and eternity. In due course, the Campas
came to be as calmly at peace in the knowledge of the truth
as they had previously been trembling in fear as a result of ignorance.

Just as the forest-dweller wants a God for his soul, so he
wants a cure for his sickness. Not that the Indian is afraid of
pain, which he faces with admirable fortitude and resignation.
But he has an awesome fear of sickness, for he has learned that
sickness often ends in death. To him the thought of death is
terrifying, even the death of another person, for the haunting
powers of the spirit of another are almost as frightening as the
prospect of his own death.

An Indian said to me, "Señora, your friend Moreno is
dead." I was both surprised and grieved. All that I knew was
that he had gone from our post to the far interior weeks before. We held a brief memorial service for him. Three days
later another Indian came from the upriver region to tell us
that my friend Moreno was very, very ill. I summoned the
first Indian and asked him why he had told me Moreno was
dead, while I had now learned that he was only very ill. The
Indian shrugged his shoulders and said that he was anticipating
the event, that he supposed that by the time he reported the
matter, Moreno would indeed be dead. When the Indians discovered that Moreno was dying, they covered him with green
leaves and left him to accomplish his demise in solitude. It is

not the fashion to stay even with one's best friend until he dies. The comfort of green leaves is the last gesture of friendliness when death threatens. That is heathenism. And that is what we had come to change through the power of the Christian Gospel.

If Moreno was still alive we might yet save him. So I called for a volunteer to go with remedies, as we could not at the time leave the post. When Marinca responded I felt a sense of shame, for I recalled my attitude when this volunteer first came to us. He was older than the other Indians, and had been not only uncouth but filthy. One eye had been lost to an enemy's arrow and he tried to conceal this with some of his long bangs. When he applied for school I confided to my husband that he was much too old and stupid to learn.

In our jungle school the curriculum included the practical things of life. So we kept a copy of the Bible at hand, and open to a page bearing a verse with the word "whosoever" in it. That word was underscored and was often referred to when we encountered an individual who seemed entirely beyond the reach of spiritual help. Sometimes I was the one to direct my husband's attention to it, but when Marinca sought entrance to the school, I was the one who had to be reminded of the verse.

My task was not easy. Each time I leaned over the dirty Indian to guide his hand in writing I had to enter the cloud of gnats that surrounded him. So dull was he that I almost despaired of teaching him anything. One night when I was developing some pictures, I invited Marinca to come into the bungalow and watch me bring his likeness to the plain white card I put into the solution. When he saw himself as he had many times in the clear water from his canoe, he was perfectly amazed.

As he left to take these great new thoughts to his campfire for pondering, I asked him if he could not believe our teaching, and told him that if he would accept it, he would have a new life reproduced as definitely as his likeness had appeared on the blank paper. He went away dubiously shaking his head, remarking that he could not see how it could be true.

Many moons later Marinca saw, not with his one physical eye only, but with the eyes of faith, that it could be true. Abounding gladness filled his heart; his mind was at peace; and he became a delight to everyone. And regeneration wrought renovation, for the day came when he was not only right within, but a well-groomed man without.

It was this Marinca who was now telling me that he would take the remedies to the suffering Moreno. At the same time he could give him food for his soul, for his own heart was full of love and light.

But Marinca arrived only to find that Moreno had died, despite the most strenuous efforts of the witch doctor to save him. That demon-possessed person had tortured two little children to death in the vain attempt to propitiate the spirits and effect the cure of the sick man.

The Campas do not believe in germs, contagion, or disease. Evil spirits cause all sickness, and cure is accomplished only when the evil spirit which is causing the trouble can be persuaded to go away. To accomplish this often a child is tortured. Because of this cruel practice, there is no lack of welcome for an orphan into a home, for orphans may be substituted for a man's own children as objects of torture.

The practice is revolting in the extreme. First, the witch doctor gives to the child tea brewed from a jungle growth to make it convulsively ill. If the healing of the sick adult is not accomplished, then the child is tortured with stones, sticks, and cruel hands. As a climax to the attempt to effect a cure the body of the child is shot full of arrows and burned. If the sick adult dies, a second child is sacrificed in the same fashion. On many occasions we have pointed out to the Campas that they are decimating their tribe by killing several children only to see the adult die, anyway. We have asked them if such practices ever saved a life. Their only defense is that they cannot just stand by and see a man die. They must do what they can, and this is the only thing they know to do.

Marinca did not return alone, but was accompanied by nine men in his dugout canoe. To my query as to why they came, they said that Marinca had persuaded them to come and listen to the teaching we had given him.

We always received visitors on the back porch of our mission house, for the door of the dispensary was there, and most callers required medical help for their many hurts and ailments. There were snake bites new and old, malaria fever, and all varieties of afflictions from itching skins to aching teeth. Usually we could help them, and by acts of kindness cause them to remain with us to learn the things we had gone to them to teach.

As I went from one to another of Marinca's men, I listened to the story they all helped to tell—the tale of the death of Moreno and of the torturing of the little boy and girl. They had seen one small body placed on top of the other, and both burned on the river bank while the crazed mother shrieked in helpless anguish nearby. She had no voice in the seizing and torturing of her children; it was the decision of the witch doctor alone. The sick man himself had nothing to say about it, either. At such times the witch doctor takes over completely, and his word is final. Anyone who opposes him is killed.

I grew faint as I listened to the sickening narrative, and even as I administered help an unworded prayer was rising from my heart. I was asking God not to permit the cruel man who was the self-appointed witch doctor in this case ever to come to the station, for I felt then that I wanted neither to help nor teach him. Later I learned that even while I prayed, I was

bandaging the hands that had been injured in the killing of
the children, for the witch doctor was one of that group telling the story. And the strange thing is that he believed he had
done right, that he had done what he could. The awful and
wicked imaginations of these hearts and minds can be understood only in the light of prevailing ignorance and superstition.

One day down river from us, a sly half-breed took an
Indian girl to be an added wife at his camp. The brother of the
Indian girl, outraged at the act, demanded that his sister be returned, informing the half-breed that unless his sister was
returned by high noon the next day, he would kill him. The
girl was not returned, and at noon two men dropped dead,
one with an arrow through his heart, and the other from the
blast of a shotgun.

The women and children belonging to the two slain men
automatically became the legal possession of other men standing by. A cold-eyed, cruel-hearted Indian took a woman and
her two children, brought them in his dugout to our clearing,
then proceeded up another river to attend to some other
violent business, saying he would come for them later.

The children were a brother and sister. The girl was
about the size of our daughter, Marilyn, and I wanted to be
kind to her. But every time I tried to touch her, she would
scream and dart away. This she would do if I so much as
spoke to her. After several days of this, our daughter came
to me one morning clutching the grimy hand of the little
forest girl in her own small hand. The battle was over; love
had cast out fear.

I put kerosene on the girl's hair, and soap and water over
the rest of her body. Then I dressed her in some of Marilyn's
clothing and they became playmates. They had their evening
meals together, their tea parties together, and for weeks they
were bosom companions.

Then one day the Indian returned and demanded the

woman and her two children. In those early years on the post we could not alter the ways of the jungle people. We had to wait for time to do its work. But this was one of those days when I longed to break their forest code, and forbid the thing which to them was legally right. Nevertheless, I had to permit him to take the three away from our clearing, and up the branch river to the place where the two children had been tortured to death.

For nights after hearing this story, it seemed in my restlessness that I lived beside the tragic scene, that I reached toward the mother trying to comfort her. We felt their woes keenly, for we loved the people of the tribe.

They needed our help, our comfort, our Saviour, for when they became Christians they discontinued their heathenish practices. Things we could never have made them do in our own power, they did voluntarily when they accepted our faith. We had the Bible, and we had medicines, and with these their needs were met. As time moved on, enlightened medical treatment replaced the witch doctor's futile cruelties, and the truth revealed in the Scriptures offered the light of faith to dispel the fearsome dread of dark nights and a Godless eternity.

The Christians were in the vanguard in the mission clearing. When they accepted our teaching they forbade anyone to practice the old ways on the property. If they wanted to live the old way they would have to go into the far interior. The believers wanted us to forget that they had ever been low and dirty and wicked. We never told them that we remembered.

CANINE CAREER

T HE EXPLORER had informed us that there were no dogs in the jungle to which we were going and that dogs would be very important in the forest world. So while our son was growing to the mature age of five months in lovely Miraflores, we went shopping for dogs. The owners of fine dogs, supposing our pockets to be full of North American gold, eagerly solicited our patronage. We waited for the offspring of a magnificent German police dog that was beautiful in every line of her sensitive body. She was a canine queen, and we wanted one of her valuable pups. It was not necessary to have many fine dogs, but it was important to have many dogs.

We named her puppy Laddie, and when he was forty-three days old we took him with us into the jungle. He chafed at the limitations of the train and the two days of auto travel, but when once we reached the mountain trail, each day increased his doggish enthusiasm for living. He would bound over the mountain paths in a pioneer exploration of everything, afraid of nothing, but terrifying me with his fearless daring. Once when running at the feet of my mule, he disappeared out of sight on a ledge so narrow that a stone struck by the foot of my mount went plunging over the cliff into the gorge below. Just one day of this nerve-racking procedure was all I could stand.

At the end of the first day's trail Perez, the mule driver, offered to become responsible for the small dog during the rest of the trip. Laddie registered resentment when we started out ahead of the cargo mules in the morning, but perfect delight crowded each hour's experience as he exhausted himself in challenging the sources of every sound and the producer of every motion. When the little fellow became too weary to walk, the good-hearted Spaniard dismounted and draped the limp dog over his saddle, where Laddie rode until wiggle returned to his eager body. When he arrived at camp each evening, he would practically collapse on the first piece of clothing the master put down for him, and there he would sleep until morning. One night, too weary to wait, he retired on a muddy boot.

The end of the journey was the beginning of forest life, and Laddie quickly developed into a big reliable animal valuable almost beyond the measure of money. He seemed to decide his own relationship to each of us. He was protector of my baby, servant of my husband, and owner of me. No stranger could approach me without Laddie's permission. He would stand in motionless restraint under his master's touch until released at a worded command to carry out instructions with amazing precision. He could be left in charge of our small son, and not a finger could touch him.

Laddie policed the clearing. When night fell and the campfires burned brighter to furnish their share of protection, the dog canvassed the entire clearing and reported the presence of snakes. He seemed to hate snakes as much as I did, but while my reaction was to flee from them his was to drive them away. He barked at leopards with the whining announcement of the presence of a detested and feared enemy. Dogs are bait for leopards, and have no chance in a fight with the huge jungle cats.

After finishing his nightly beat Laddie would return to camp, rub his nose against my hand extended to him from beneath the mosquito tent, and report that everything was right. He slept beneath our baby's little white-screened bed which doubled for a play-pen by day. When our bungalow was completed and we hooked the screened door, Laddie dug a hole in the ground directly under the floor where the baby's bed was placed, and there he slept. When the nursery was installed in the opposite corner of the building, on the very first night we heard the dog's heavy tail striking the stringers under the house as he crossed to the opposite corner, located the position of David's bed, made a new hole in the ground, and went to sleep as usual under baby's bed. He was not easily dismissed from duty.

One day while out hunting with an Indian, a leopard leaped on Laddie and gripped his neck between vicious jaws before the hunter could kill him. Laddie came home with body badly swollen, and so stiff he could turn his head only by turning his whole body. When he had crossed the river to reach the camp, he found that one of our tall hounds, Fido, stood howling on the other side of the water. Fido was a good dog but afraid of water. Never in all his life had he crossed the river except when swimming at Laddie's side. After only a brief pause, Laddie swam back to the other side of the river and escorted Fido across. From the distance we had not observed the injury our favorite dog had suffered, but we esteemed him even more highly when we knew of this act while in physical pain, an act of faithfulness to a friend.

For weeks we fought for Laddie's life. Infection set in which required poulticing, lancing, draining, and medications which we provided as if for a human adult. Eventually he recovered, but for a long time he lost his zest for hunting. Later, however, he again led the pack into the forest to bring out the wanted prey.

Gringa was the mother of the beautiful family that could have made Laddie very proud. His only concern was that they be proper dogs, and he trained them with strong supervision. Gringa was a thoroughbred, but too fine for the jungle, and we lost her.

Chico and Dinah were strong big hounds that increased the pack. When the pack fell below seventeen it was serious. While a good dog is only bait for the prowling leopards, a pack of dogs will bravely join their barking forces to keep the jungle cats at a distance.

Chico died the violent death of the snake-bitten, thus proving the fatal effects of the poison of that particular snake. He had shaken many snakes to death, but a jergon ended the boisterous life of the daring hound. Fido and many others of the family lived adventurous lives and died tragic deaths.

Dogs and monkeys find friendship difficult. Mickie was our favorite monkey. He was a tiny tease, and the dogs could not endure him. He was welcomed by none of the dogs but Laddie, and that perhaps because we petted them both together. Mickie was so tiny that his bedroom was a pound coffee tin lined with purple velvet. One day he ran across the top of my stove and burned the palm of each tiny foot. I nursed them back to usefulness, but I never risked his unguarded presence in my kitchen again. He seemed not to know that there was danger in a stove.

At the carpenter bench the tiny monkey would attempt to pick up any item the workman laid down. One day he started to suck the juice from a lime-lemon fruit of which we were very fond. A convulsive shudder shook his small body. He backed away from the piece of fruit with a quizzical glance at the man who had put it down, and then started to suck it again with grim determination. Eventually he learned to enjoy it, and expected his portion when one was cut.

No one blamed the dogs for not liking Mickie. He invited himself to share their food, and when snapped at would jump to the back of a dog's neck and pull and chatter in a most annoying fashion. The dogs in turn would snarl and strike, but find it impossible to defend themselves against him. Laddie was the only dog that would permit Mickie to eat from his plate. But one day the tiny monk was too annoying even for him, and in an attempt to teach him a needed lesson, Laddie picked him up and shook him as he often did his own offspring. But Mickie was too delicate for such handling. When Laddie put him down, Mickie folded his tiny arms, put his wee head on them and passed out.

It was pathetic to watch Laddie try to revive him. He nudged him, fretted over him, and finally as if in shamed despair went away for several hours. When he returned, it was to the place where he had last seen the little monkey. Missing him, he came to us wistfully, as if trying to apologize for what he had done.

Laddie introduced us to many interesting animals. His barking one day took us across the river to observe our first anteater. This mammal had dug his vicious claw through an ant hill, laid his long sticky tongue across the track of the claw, and waited until the ants had defiantly swarmed over the length of it. Then he pulled in his tongue which was coated with a complete dinner.

In a similar manner we met our first sloth. Laddie snarled and barked, using a combination of the sounds he employed to announce both man and beast. Perhaps he scarcely knew whether this was the one or the other. When my husband shot the creature he said it was more like shooting a man than an animal, for the color of its face, and its expression and pattern, were so nearly human. These slow, lazy creatures which make it a practice to walk upside down along the under side of a limb are most interesting.

Together, the Indians and Laddie brought me many pets. One day it was a tiny deer with painted spots and a baby cry, whose mother had been killed by the hunter. We brought it up on a bottle, then released it when it was large enough to enjoy jungle life.

We raised a paujil in a wired enclosure. The paujil is the largest bird in the jungle and when full grown is comparable to a year-old domestic turkey. How we came to get him was this: One day when our David had become quite expert under the instruction of the Indians, he shot the paujil with his bow and arrow, pinning his wing securely to his body. Terror-stricken, David called us to save the screaming bird. The bird was not much hurt, but our young Nimrod learned in the future not to shoot at anything he was not aiming to kill.

One night the Indian custodian of the canoes came with Laddie to report that a boa was wrapped around the tree to which the dugouts were tied. When Ross shot the creature, it fell from the tree, and we discovered that it was not a boa, but a five-foot animal resembling a giant lizard. These are reasonably common, but unreasonably ugly, the only pretty thing about them being their bronze green color. His saw-tooth shape, from the head to the end of the tail, resembles the dragon on a Chinese vase, and when you have seen one you can believe almost any weird dragon story.

There was a time in our early experience in the jungle when the Indians were tangled in tribal and inter-tribal warfare, in fact were angry with everyone. This created an emergency, for we depended on wild game for our meat. The Indians would not hunt for us, and my husband dared not leave the station. As though Laddie intuitively understood the conditions, he took it upon himself to hunt for us. For more than five months we had no game except that which the dogs brought, yet we were never without a supply.

Laddie would lead the dogs into the forest upstream from our post, and back into the branch river beds where there was only a trickling of water. There, enjoying the tender green growths, he would come upon a deer, which he would gently encourage to go toward the big river. Then from our place we would recognize the high yelping call he used only when pursuing deer. The hunter would grab his rifle, paddle upstream in his dugout, bag the deer, and bring it to the clearing.

Sometimes the deer would reach the big river ahead of the hunter, cross, and disappear into the jungle on the other side. Laddie would follow, circle, and bring it back. If the current was strong, the deer would come down stream seeking a place to cross, with Laddie following just near enough to take a nip from time to time as a smart reminder to the deer that he was being followed. I have watched this performance from the river bank with field glasses, and marveled at the ingenuity of this dog. Down at the port Laddie would circle the deer and bring him ashore at the spot where his master waited. Ross quickly dressed the animal and presented me with steaks to be prepared for dinner. We ate our meat those days thankful to God and a good dog.

Perhaps Laddie would not have seemed so wonderful to us if we had known him only in civilization, for there we would not have needed him so much. His service would have been performed in the homeland by organized labor, public servants, friends, authorities and officers. But there were none of these out there.

He had a part in all the pleasures and dangers that touched our lives. When the family paddled away in a dugout, perhaps to cross the river in quest of a bunch of bananas, Laddie was with us. He would ride in the boat for a while, then splash into the river and swim ahead, as if desiring to welcome us on the other shore. He had the rare gift of leadership, and appeared to be in full control of the situation at all times. It was a quality we could not but admire.

GALLERY PIECES

Hung in focused light on the walls of my memory's gallery are a few pictures reproduced from life originals. As I gaze upon them from time to time, the conviction grows on me that no young person can consider himself too well qualified for missionary service, that the very best in any of us is none too good to offer God for use in His high and holy service.

The ugliness, sacrifice, and drudgery involved in missionary experience are so dramatized by returned missionaries in their reports, that the listener may fail to behold the beauty which rightfully should be painted into the picture. An appreciation of the magnificent will help the missionary volunteer to grasp a grandeur that should become visible both to the natural and spiritual eye.

On many occasions, for example, we have stepped from a hovel in the mountains almost sick from breathing air that was heavy with disease and the nauseating smell of rotting flesh into another world of light and beauty where we could inhale deeply of the clear fresh breeze and quickly recover from the misery within. Before us was a splendor of flame and purple painting the sunset skies. Turning, we could see a gold and pearl brilliance reflected on snow-topped ranges to the east. The ugliness within spoke of the wages of sin and death, but the glory without was a prophecy of a beauty far beyond the contaminations of man.

It was not until we had paid the utmost farthing—had turned our backs on the protection of government, the comforts of civilization, and the fellowship of friends that we found this isolated post of glory at the end of the trail. The post itself offered none of these things. Once the government warned us that hostile Indians were on the march bent on staging a massacre at our post, but offered no help. We were simply instructed to flee for our lives. "Why," asked an army official incredulously, as he rested on our veranda, "do you stay here in the midst of such rigors? The cost is too great; you have nothing that really makes life worth while."

The officer meant well; he merely lacked the capacity to see. His heart had never sung with the enchantment of a tropical morning, when the ebony trees burst into a bouquet of canary flowers. He did not know the beauty of a fawn stepping gracefully through the silver ferns at the edge of our clearing. He had never responded to the sound of dipping paddles, as a dugout shoved off from our river bank to carry red men to others of their tribe with the glorious message of the Gospel.

Of course the cost was great. Many times tears fell on my hands as I stirred tasteless mixtures, cooking food over hot wood fires. Often my body ached from hours of such routine duties as peeling yuca root, washing dishes in muddy water, sweeping down bats that hung like bunches of grapes under the edges of our crude breakfast table, poulticing brown hands and feet in which thorns seemed to have become inextricably embedded, fighting for the life of the red woman's tiny babe only to see it expire in my hands. I wept, fearing that my own baby would grow up without a mother, for I felt that I could never survive such pioneering experiences.

But at sunset, when I knelt in the ashes at the campfire and discerned the light of understanding flash in the black eyes of a forest woman, my compensation began, and when I felt the pressure of her hand in mine and heard her voice declare her faith in my God, I quickly forgot the pain of the day in an ecstacy which was almost divine.

There is no week in the jungle. There is only a moon, and then another moon. But a week had to be established if we were to have a Lord's Day, and that was no simple innovation. For the red men had always hunted when they wanted to, worked only when they must, rested when they liked, and gone nowhere at any specific time. From a life entirely free of regulation, we taught the Indians to attend church on Sunday until noon, and to spend the afternoon in quiet friendliness. Classes were conducted during the forenoons on Mondays through Fridays, when we explained the mysteries of letters and figures, and the art of reading the Bible. Saturdays were devoted to the hunt, in order that the campfires throughout the clearing might be supplied with game.

One day while standing on the river bank, I saw an Indian all but drown a girl whom he wanted for his wife. To one of the older Indians standing near I protested, "You would not stand by and let him drown her, would you?" At which he merely shrugged his bare shoulders and observed, "She should be willing to become his wife." This was simply social custom, the red man's way of proposing marriage to her—to make her willing to accompany him to his campfire and become his wife. This one proved to be unwilling and fought her way free. She remained near me for some days, and eventually became the wife of a man on whom already she had fixed her desires. Later the one who seemed bent on drowning her took another girl for his wife, and the two couples dwelt as good neighbors near my campfire. Both lived happily forever afterward!

On another occasion an Indian with a formidable record of killings called at our place while my husband was up river with another missionary putting the launch in dry dock for repairs. I opened the screen door of the veranda where my missionary friend and I had been doing hand work and invited him to sit with us. The killer asked me a few ingenuous questions to see if I recognized him and when he knew I did, he asked if I were not afraid of him. Recognizing a very real danger, while I continued the conversation, my friend waved a towel from the door to attract the attention of our husbands. Since we did not use the deer horn, they realized they were needed and so came on the double. At this the killer remained only to trade some balls of raw rubber for a few small items he liked and went away. A few weeks later he returned with a burning fever, and quite unmindful of the past, my husband attended him through a long illness. It was by such acts of kindness, of returning good for evil, that we attempted to sow good seed which might in God's gracious providence bear fruit unto life eternal.

This prayer, recently popularized by Peter Marshall, was daily ours,

"God, give us grace to endure that which cannot be changed—
  Courage to change that which should be changed—
  And wisdom to know the one from the other."

Apart from the Indians, our only neighbors were a half-breed with his family up river, and another half-breed with his family down river. Both of these were sons of convicts who had fled Europe, buried themselves in the Peruvian jungles beyond the reach of the law, and taken Indian wives. We scarcely knew how to pray for these two neighbors, although we were anxious to win them to faith in the Christ they needed so desperately. To show our friendship we welcomed them to our camp, had them at our table, permitted them to mingle with our Indians, gave them gifts from our meager store, and supplied them with remedies when they were ill.

Although the neighbor down river pretended to be our friend, and the friend of our Indians, he was in fact most deceitful and wicked. After eating our food, and pretending to approve our teaching, he would mingle with our Indians and tell them that we would deceive and rob them, and throw them into slavery. He constantly promoted confusion.

After faithfully witnessing to this half-breed for a number of years, we could not see that we had effected any improvement in him at all. For a long stretch of time he would be most gracious, appear at our table, declare himself our friend, and help us through serious difficulties. But always he would revert to his false accusations, bitter denunciations, and evil conduct. Evidently God's Spirit ceased to strive with him, for one day we found him with an arrow in his heart from the bow of an Indian whose sister he had stolen.

Since our half-breed neighbor up river was openly our enemy, he could be more easily dealt with. It was on his porch that we had slept on our way into the jungle, and it was he who had told us of the leopard which jumped across the bodies of two men to seize a dog. Repeatedly he had visited our station and accepted our aid, only to go away and publicly demonstrate hatred of us. Doubtless he realized that our Gospel would end his wicked traffic. In a sudden outburst, he one day leaped from a chair on our veranda, and pressing a revolver against my husband's throat, threatened that unless he left the country at once, he would kill him.

When the authorities in Iquitos became convinced that this half-breed had murdered two members of his family, they decided to investigate. For some years they had known of his violence, but they left him in the hands of the Indians, feeling that in due course they would take care of him in their own way. So it was that two armed officers appeared on the mail launch, went on two days beyond us up river, and returned with the man a prisoner in chains.

This mail launch was our only contact with the outside world, and its appearance was always hailed with enthusiasm. While my husband entered the cabin with the captain to exchange mail, our son, David, with a number of small Indian boys, viewed the activities from the river's bank.

One of the Indian boys recognized the half-breed aboard ship and pointed him out to the other boys. David had overheard this man's threat to his father, and had not forgotten. But he mistook one of the officers who bore a pistol at his belt for the potential killer.

When this man, uniformed and with pistol in plain view left the launch and started up the hillside toward our bungalow, David immediately surmised that he was bent on murder. He thought he was coming to the house to attack me first, and with all his boyish protective instincts aroused, he sprinted through the undergrowth to reach the house first.

Sobbing, he breathlessly poured forth his story. Of course when the uniformed officer appeared, I recognized David's mistake. But it was not until the officers had accepted our invitation to remain for dinner, and had assured David that the wicked man would be safely put in prison that he again was at ease.

Missionary effort seems to be a one-sided race between the man of sin, who with fastidious dress and adequate equipment travels the easy path, and the witness of truth who must almost bare-handed fight his way through the jungle entanglements of ignorance and error. Our work was never easy; perhaps that is why God permitted us to witness so many brilliant victories and such glorious triumphs. It has seemed at times as if all the world's galleries scarcely could exhibit all the master-pieces of the works of God He permitted us to behold with our own eyes.

We never had to waste any time speculating as to whether there would be storms in the jungle; every May and October violent winds recurred with scientific precision. I was always nervous in anticipation of them, for if our bungalow should be destroyed there was no other shelter, and if either of us was killed, the other would be desolate.

One day as I was reaching for something on my pantry shelf, I was halted as by the hand of the Lord, while an inner voice assured me that I need not continue in fear of the ap-proaching storm. When the storm struck, I watched as the walls of our house seemed to breathe with the repeated winds, and the floor to heave. For the sake of ventilation, we had left screened transom spaces on all sides of the bungalow, with the roof extending considerably beyond. Yet the winds drove with such force that the rains dashed into and completely across the interior of the building. But neither this storm, nor any other, ever seriously damaged our little home.

Nevertheless, we braced ourselves against the wind that soon came like a giant, elbowing his way through the palm and ebony forest. Never shall I forget that sight. The whole jungle world seemed aware of its power. Small wild animals scurried through the clearing, and a doe hurried past us to the river's edge where she paused momentarily, then swam across, leaving an ever-widening track on the river's surface. At the other edge of the water she paused again as if to get her bear-ings, then made her way directly to where a tiny fawn had probably already called, "Mother!"

Parrots accelerated their chatter to high screeching, as the voices of Indians rose with the excitement of the approach-ing storm. Monkeys reached for their babies that were too far alimb for safety, and night birds hushed their warblings and sought shelter in heavy foliage against strong limbs. Indians shoved logs closer together to strengthen fires. Slender trees became whips in the hand of the wind. Tall ebonies were stripped of their petal dresses, while palms were reduced to ribboned shreds. The earth alone was still.

Rain drops plowed the soil, forming craters and lifting puffs of dust like volcanic smoke. Our young son and daughter caught at flying leaves and petals, and laughed their appreciation as though a fancied drama had broken into reality especially for their delight. They were not afraid and were reluctant to go inside and to bed.

First drops were quickly followed by a pounding torrent which caused the surface of the broad river to lift as water met water. Lightning illuminated the destruction, while thunder roared like cannon through the forest.

At daybreak we could see the full effect of the storm. It had swept along two sides of our clearing just inside the uncut forest, mowing a path avenue-wide where trees were flattened as though they had been grass. But our property, lying in the protective curve of the storm's path, was unharmed. It seemed to be a symbol of our whole program. The winds of opposing forces had many times threatened to destroy the entire project. Heavy gales of wrath had blown against us from almost every direction. But always when the storm subsided we were in the curve of the protecting arm of God, and even greater progress was made.

We cut the trees left standing between our clearing and the path of the storm, and with what the wind had done, the cleared acreage was much larger. We could but bow our heads in thanksgiving to Him who had made even a fierce storm our benefactor.

At some seasons the forest assumed the aspect of a beautiful painting, with flowers spread over the rounded heads of the

ebony trees, and across the broad shoulders of other forest
giants. Plumes of coral and bells of scarlet covered the tops
of other trees, making them appear like miniature garden
spots when viewed from our crow's-nest on the river bank.
Every year I tried to raise domestic flowers, but they refused
to blossom; it seemed that God put the jungle flowers on the
trees as a sort of compensation.

In childhood trees had been my friends. They became almost like people with a distinct personality—one especially, a
giant whose roots spread half above ground to form natural
treasure chests and secret vaults for maps and charts of pretended value. Even a coffee-maker was there, into which we
poured dried dock seeds stripped from weed stems.

Here in the jungle we grew real coffee, and I was especially fond of the coffee trees. That was why I selected one
as our Christmas tree; for instruction in Christian truth it became a happy medium. The tree could tell the story of Christmas, but much more—the story of creation both of man and
trees, the identification of Christ as the true creator, and life
everlasting as typified by the evergreen. In the absence of
hemlock or spruce, our tree adorned with red and green
coffee beans was a satisfactory substitute.

At my childhood home we niched steps up one side of a
fallen tree trunk and down the other. These became a part of
our jaunts into the woods, where mother taught us to contruct
swings from branches of trees by weaving the ends together
for a seat. She also taught us to distinguish harmless from
noxious growths, mushrooms from poisonous toadstools, and
how to deaden pain from a bumblebee sting by the application
of mud. Now these things sprang to life. In the jungle I found
myself teaching my own children the wiles of the forest, and
how to enjoy the good and avoid the dangerous.

Tragedies that were near-misses—that could have been
but were not—would make another series of gallery pieces.

Late one afternoon an Indian arrived with a whole fist full of battle-front dispatches: the Campas were on the march, a massacre was planned, tonight our place would be burned and all of us would be killed.

In planning the protection of my child that night, I decided to hide him between a chest of drawers and an inside wall. Then with feminine inconsistency, I prayed that if the attack came and Ross and I were killed, that God would permit an arrow to find its way past the obstruction, lest David fall into the hands of these savages.

The invaders approached by the river, but passed without staging an attack. What caused them to change their minds we did not know, but we believed, as did our Indian monitor, that God had overshadowed the clearing that night. How He did it—by angel's wing, wall of fire, or unseen host, we did not know. The important fact was—we were delivered.

On another occasion, my husband and two Indians traveled from early morning until late in the day, conscious that a leopard was keeping step with them. Although the animal was concealed on the opposite side of a narrow ravine, they expected him to vault it at any moment.

The party had set out on a preaching tour to carry the Gospel to the hinterland, yet they were well armed. With arms they obtained meat and with arms they protected themselves.

When deepening shadows warned the travelers that they must soon make camp, they felt they had better assume the offensive. Actually, they had little choice, for at a sharp turn in the ravine they came face to face with him, all set for action. He was crouching, with jaws open for business. A bullet from a heavy rifle quickly ended the threat, and camp was made far enough removed from where the leopard lost his coat to avoid prowlers of the night. It was hoped that other callers would content themselves with the carcass of the animal.

But now—a different picture. Perhaps the most lonely woman I ever met was the one who gazed into my face as though she were studying the pages of a magazine—who touched my hands as if she had waited an entire lifetime to do it, although she had never seen me before.

We had been eleven hours in the saddle, traversing mountain ridges and bridgeless rivers, penetrating our way into the jungle. It was on our first trip, and David was an infant. He was healthy and happy, and fretted only when occasionally his cooing tangled with a sob. Then knowing that we dared not stop, for we must be off the trail by dark, I would long to get my child into my arms to comfort him. I would sing, "Rock-a-bye, Baby" to the tune of "Blessed Assurance," and it worked like a specific.

For two whole days it had rained and while baby things could be washed, to dry them was impossible. Consequently, the state of the laundry was serious when that night we arrived at the small palm shelter and gleaming campfire. The lonely woman had been that way for years. True, she had known happier days, but that was long ago. Now she was with her husband stationed at one of the most remote outposts on the government trail.

She presented to me an interesting proposition. If I would only stay awake and talk to her, she would iron my baby's clothes, hang them on heavy cords near her fire, and then iron them again. She assured me that if we did this all night, she would have the entire lot dry by morning. What I talked about she did not care, but I must talk. It was a strange but promising proposal, so although weariness had wrung my body to limpness, I jumped at the offer. And I must confess that I have seldom had so appreciative an audience. What did I talk about? Well, among the many things of my discourse were some which I trust have made her less lonely.

BLACK WINGS

ORCHIDS, BEGONIAS, and fantastically precise clinging vines that grow a leaf to the left of the stem, then one to the right in exact, waxed perfection were probably made to grow in the jungle to help you forget the pests. It sometimes seemed to me that when the pernicious things were allotted to earth's areas, a great leftover quantity was disposed of in the tropics. But that is not true. The common house-fly, for instance, is not known in the jungle.

When our bungalow was erected, though there were no house-flies, vampire bats invaded the attic between our cedar ceiling and the galvanized roof. They fluttered on wing-tipped voyages above our ceiling, all through the night every night, in maddening reminder of their restless presence. While one crew returned from nibbling the scalps of tiny babies and fingers and toes of older folks, another went forth to fasten themselves on cattle. I abhorred them.

A raincoat that had hung against a bamboo wall for several days was very heavy when it was lifted from its peg. The Indian boy to whom the coat was handed for inspection removed thirty-seven small bats from the inside folds and sleeves.

You soon learn in the jungle that you should never put your arms into the sleeves of anything without first investigating whether there is some living thing inside.

You never open an umbrella over your head, but hold it away from you as far as possible and lift it gingerly to permit the scorpion to drop to the ground instead of down your neck. You never use a bath towel without first checking to see if a spider is hidden inside. When you take off your shoe at the end of the day you may discover in it a squashed cockroach if you failed to shake your shoes well before putting them on.

A recent magazine article reported the discovery of vampire bats in the Peruvian jungles with a twenty-six inch wingspread. But it is not the size, it is the way of the vampire that concerns us.

Our bungalow was planned to keep out as many annoying things as possible, but we never were able to exclude the vampires from our attic. When it seemed that we had closed every transom and air space, they still crept through crevices.

We learned the subtle ways of the vampire before we had cedar walls and copper screens about us, when mosquito tents were our sole protection. Jungle nights are hot, and one does not pull down the net until he is about to fall asleep, lest he miss a breath of air. When wearied by the blazing heat and conflict of the day, and occupied with thoughts of the morrow, coolness and rest are welcome. Suddenly one becomes conscious that the gentle brush of a passing breeze is being repeated in a measured fanning that eases breathing. Wearied body and relaxed mind welcome the presence of a slight wind from the river, or is it some thoughtful person, who passing the hammock has noted that you are practically breathing your last, and stopped to pick up a broad leaf to fan you? You do not open your eyes to discover the answer, for if there are those who care enough to fan you, you are grateful. If they should feel that you are even strong enough to open your eyes, they might go away—and fan themselves.

But if you had opened your eyes, you would have discovered that it was no such friendly visitor, but a vampire bat which had stationed himself in mid-air above you. There he was holding his altitude by rapid vibrations of his silken wings; this created the stirring of the atmosphere. However, it feels so good that you keep your eyes closed, and yield yourself to the pleasantness, regardless of the source. In refreshed drowsiness you hear a lullaby—hmmm, hmmmmm, hmmmmm, a gentle murmur which lulls you into sweet repose. Again, if you had opened your eyes to observe the singer, you would have recognized the vampire which had won you to yieldedness by his refreshing allurements, now so close that the hum of his wings is like music.

Startled by a sudden shock that speaks of danger, you languidly reason that even though it was a malarial mosquito, the damage is done and there is nothing you can do about it. So you sink back into oblivion. Had you aroused yourself at the signal of danger, you would have seen that the vampire had boldly pressed two tiny needle-like teeth into your flesh, and even after the warning pain had subsided, the teeth had not been withdrawn, but a hungry mouth had opened over the teeth, and your blood was being lapped away.

Someone from another hammock may have warned you that a vampire was about, but you had never been hurt by one and so neglected to lower the protecting tent. The delightful fanning deceived you, and invited repose to the strains of music. Though for a moment you were startled by the painful warning, you slept on.

If someone concerned for your welfare did not observe your plight and awaken you, then you would continue to sleep on. Even when awakened, your drowsy attitude may mean merely your wish to be left alone; you are cool for the first time since coming to the tropics; completely relaxed for the first time in weeks; nothing hurts you; you feel no need of arousing yourself. You may languidly open your eyes and glance at the vampire, but by now your dulled senses counsel that it is nothing to fear. So you close your eyes and a deadly enemy does its work.

Many of my jungle experiences held a gem of spiritual truth which I did not at the time fully appreciate. But as time passed, and distance gave better perspective, I came to realize that there was far more to them than at first appeared.

How like those lulled into a false sense of security by the vampire are my Indian friends. They have listened to the song of the siren until they have been almost literally transformed into beasts. First they merely heard the voice of ease and pleasure, little realizing what would be the end when the enemy had completed his work.

The Campas have been hypnotized by the vampire for centuries, so long indeed that they are now entirely insensible either to his purposes or designs. The evil one has done his work surreptitiously, never revealing himself as the vicious, soul-destroying thing that he actually is. In the distant past he doubtless appeared to these simple folk as both benevolent and attractive, but when their senses were thoroughly deadened, he left them deluded dupes, entirely powerless under his spell.

The Indians sleep near their fires for protection from violent nocturnal enemies, for they have discovered that light keeps them away. But there is another Light, another darkness, another vampire, and He who is the Sun of righteousness must rise if the gloom of sin is to be destroyed and the power of the great antagonist broken. Jungle paths must have the light of the Word of God, that Campas may walk, run, even leap, fearlessly and without falling. As yet few of them have heard of that lamp for their feet, or that light for their path. The vampire has anesthetized them. They sleep the long sleep of death.

FOREST FOLK

My son and I stepped out of our home for sunrise inspection of the glorious world out-of-doors. We loved the feel of morning air and sun. Every day new wonders awaited us as we examined the spider webs which strung a bridge from fern to fern. Dew jeweled the entire silver and green network, and we touched the beads and watched them roll the length of the frond and nestle in the feathery curl at the end. A few spiders which had not completed their project were trying to regain the lost time. There were dainty little spiders and ugly thick-legged ones.

Brilliantly plumed birds chirped and twittered and called, displaying their beauty in feather rather than in song. They were our friends, and we loved them. We grieved at the fall of each before the hunter's arrow, and insisted that the itinerant humming birds about our door be spared. The Indian boys skin them, use their bright feathers for adornments, and roast the tiny birds for one delicious mouthful.

Flame-streaked feathers and quantities of paint of the same hue adorned the three red men who bent over the glowing coals. I could not fail to notice them, for they had made their campfire at the very edge of the trail. As usual, it was a temporary affair, for the red man builds his fire and prepares his food where he finds his quarry or when he is hungry. There is no bothersome trip for utensils or salt; for him these do not exist.

With gleeful laughter they invited me to join them for breakfast. Since it is wise to be courteous to men of the jungle, I accepted their invitation and added myself to the circle around the fire. Almost at once I discovered my mistake. For on the menu just one item appeared—a heap of huge thick worms, each like a tomato worm, but tan-colored instead of green. You chose your worm, dropped it on the glowing coals, then watched it writhe, sizzle and pop. The popping was the signal that it was ready for eating. You retrieved it and gingerly passed a thumb and finger along its length to brush off the brittle horns and hairs. Then you broke it into delicate morsels and partook of it with great gusto—that is if you were a red man. From the delight registered on the faces of my hosts, I am sure the meal was choice.

The trail never permitted monotony. Often I was repulsed by the customs and habits of the forest people; again I was astonished and delighted with them. I wept with pity over the condition of one Indian, and grew stiff with indignation over the conduct of another. To one guilty of some heinous crime I would give an extra hour of the precious time that belonged to my rest period—the time put aside to build up a reserve for the demands of the morrow.

I watched my husband put a stamping, raging troublemaker off the mission property one day, and three months later saw him sitting on a log telling him the way of salvation. With wrath chilling my senses, I saw him calmly wipe an angry woman's spit off his face. With a heart sick with fear, I saw him throw an insulting drunken Indian into a palm shelter with instructions not to appear again until he could conduct himself like a man. Steps that usually no man would have dared take were taken in the confidence of the presence of that Invisible Power which is promised to those who stand for righteousness.

When we issued from a series of unprecedented outbreaks of wickedness we would sit back in rather breathless relief, confident that nothing quite so bad could ever recur. Then before another week had gone we were in the midst of circumstances that made the former ones seem mere shadows in comparison.

One morning I found a girl on the river bank looking more like a living corpse than anything else. There was no expression on her face or in her eyes. When I addressed her she registered neither fear nor joy.

When I heard Chiquicha's story I readily understood the reason. She was the daughter of big Ashupi and his wife, both of whom had been cruelly mistreated by a half-breed settler up the river. They were beaten and threatened at the point of a gun, but made their escape leaving their daughter behind. They reached the mission in an old dugout, bewailing the loss of their child, who was still held captive by the man up the river.

Now Chiquicha had escaped, and picked her way on foot through the jungle, fear driving her to undertake this almost impossible venture. There she sat, her senses numbed by suffering and fear, her body wasted by ill treatment and starvation. But youth has wonderful recuperative powers. Restoration to her parents, and food from their fireside, soon coaxed back her natural loveliness.

It was a delight for me to teach her of a Saviour who cares for the daughters of every race, to tell her that no trail is so remote that it cannot be found by the Christ who came "to seek and to save that which was lost."

I cannot forget the stir in my heart when I saw the new light in Barrerro's black eyes as he arose from his knees and began to preach his first sermon. It was addressed to the group of men who had been kneeling with him. He argued, seemingly as much with himself as them, that they must cease their tribal custom of robbing, torturing and killing.

All along the trail we encountered the needy ones of earth, and here was another. I found her on my very door step—old, toothless, and indescribably ugly. If she had ever known a joy in her life it certainly had left no trace of its visit.

I obeyed the impulse to sit down by her and talk, but every time I spoke her face dropped into her hands, and from there down on her knees. When I tried speaking more gently she acted the same. Fortunately David and Marilyn were playing inside the screened door, and as I turned my attention to them, the old Indian woman followed my example. Though my unexpected words had frightened her, as we watched the little ones a smile came to her face. When I again ventured to make remarks, her old head wagged in response.

Now that I had an audience, I told her of the living God and of His Son, Jesus the Saviour. I told the story swiftly, for I knew that in a few minutes the men of her party would return from the trading post, and that she would go with them over the river bank, into the dugout, and off to the depths of the forest.

I gave her a prayer to be addressed to the Living God of whom I had been speaking, a prayer in the name of His Son—for mercy, guidance and salvation. She repeated the words after me again and again, and went off with them instead of a farewell on her lips. She went as I knew she would, but we prayed that in the woods that were her home she would receive an answer from the Christ who declared, "Whosoever shall call upon the name of the Lord shall be saved."

The red race is smitten with haunting fear which super-stition pushes into their minds. We listened to Pashco's story, while terror blanched his copper face.

At dusk the red man had been paddling up river in his canoe with a large fish lying at his feet. There must be fish smoking over the night fire to provide breakfast for his family. The red man's baby was tucked away in a little hammock of vines which was swung between two branches of a tree. His wife was seated under the early stars before the fire. Suddenly a deep-throated, "khon-khon-khon" came from the direction of the yuca patch, at once wrecking the calm of the gathering darkness. Pashco, now at his home fire, stood listening intently to a voice which filled his wife and children with terror.

As the voice drew nearer, it appeared more threatening, more terrible. The Indian knows the voices of the forest and can tell you in a moment the appearance and characteristics of the animals, birds and insects he hears. But this voice they had never heard before. Was it man or beast prowling through the forest? On it came until seemingly well into the yuca patch. There it stopped, remained to rend the stillness at in-tervals throughout the night, then become distant, and finally silent as morning dawned.

The same program was repeated the next night, and the next, and the next. Other Indians gathered to try to identify this strange voice, but none returned for a second night. Each was baffled and afraid. When the family could stand it no longer, they crossed the river each night, and did not return to their home until daybreak. Strangely their house was not disturbed, nor their yuca patch robbed. So they were puzzled more than ever. Was it a cannibal from a savage tribe or a monstrous beast new to these forests? They arrived at one conclusion, that whatever it was it lived solely on grass and human beings, otherwise the yuca would have been eaten. Both man and beast eat yuca.

For weeks the haunting sound continued, until in despair Pashco decided to burn his house and make a home elsewhere. Upon hearing this another Indian counseled him to wait for one more moon, when he would himself come with a third man, and together they would tackle the intruder.

Now, this Indian father was no coward, but a brave courageous man. When he found tracks of an immense leopard in the moist earth back of his house he did not hesitate, for he knew the ways of these fierce beasts and how to fight them. He killed the leopard. When he heard shots on the river, he took his gun and went down to his dugout to await the arrival of a man he believed intended to kill a guest who was staying under his roof. Neither beast nor man did he fear, but the voice of the unknown sent shivers down his spine. Nevertheless, he accepted the wise counsel of his friend, and on the appointed night they set forth to conquer this foe.

Early the next morning they laid their enemy on our door step. What was it? Merely a fowl—an immense bird to be sure, but one whose habitat was the mountains and which never before had appeared in the jungle. He had merely wanted to taste the green of the tropics.

So ended Pashco's story and his fear of that strange voice. But Pashco and others of his tribe, whether it was superstition or not, were just as suspicious of the missionary's voice. Is that to be wondered at? For out on the trail the missionary's voice is new and strange—a voice to be doubted, suspected, and feared. It can by no means be accepted until proved harmless. No voice had ever been lifted there to tell the story of a Christ who had died to save Indians from sin, and at last to transport their souls to an eternal heaven. Could it be possible that after death their souls need not wander helplessly through the forests for all eternity? Because the message of the missionary was so new and strange, it took patience and persistence to win these forest dwellers.

BLUE CHINA

IN MY youth I caught a fleeting vision of missions, but it came to me when I was not yet capable of entertaining a heart passion. It was mainly emotional in character, leaving an impression of stars, the Orient, and brown hands lifted in fervent but hopeless supplication to the heavens. God's ambassador was not a human being of warm flesh and blood like me, but some sort of celestial personage, impregnated with elements of the divine. I listened to missionary addresses in awed admiration, but I could never see myself a part of such an assignment.

My conception of foreign missions was the barrel type. Whenever a missionary was mentioned, that is a woman missionary, the curtain of my imagination arose on a fantastic creature dressed in left-overs which were packed into a barrel and sent overseas once a year—glories in which she must shine until the advent of next year's barrel. I never wanted to meet her. In fact, I winced at the thought of her.

All things foreign were distasteful to me. I was horrified by snake stories; the Spaniard's dagger and the Oriental's sword terrified me.

In due course I was to find that while missionary service has in it something of exotic beauty, the ugliness of the barrel, and the tensions of fear, yet basically it is none of these. It is a reasonable service to be rendered by human beings like you and me. Hard facts will dissipate missionary fancy; a vibrant personality will conquer "barrel" ugliness; faith will drive out fear.

Let neither glamor nor a flare for adventure draw you to the trail. Neither permit dread of danger to keep you from it if God summons you. For He who calls will cover every experience with all necessary provision.

One night after lights-out I felt something fall on my throat. I first brushed at it with my hand, then I turned my flashlight on it. There beside me was a scorpion about four inches long—a live scorpion, striking in every direction with its dagger-tipped tail. Scorpions strike the very instant they touch an object, or when anything touches them and the poison they inject results in raging fever or torturous pain. As quickly as possible I plunked my blue silk elbow pillow over it and held it prisoner until my husband came to my rescue. Then, when I had once more recovered my equilibrium, I recalled our Lord's promised protection to the seventy when He sent them forth: "Behold, I give unto you power to tread on serpents and scorpions . . . and nothing shall by any means hurt you." I felt the promise was intended for at least seventy-one!

Another night I was awakened by a sound like wings beating against the boards of the wall at the head of my bed. Flashing my light I located what disturbed me—a spider as large as a child's hand, with gleaming eyes and unbelievably long legs. I killed that one quickly, but exactly the same thing recurred eight nights in a row. After a while things like this get on the nerves. Snakes, scorpions, spiders, clothes from the barrel, daggers, swords—and yet a "reasonable service"? Certainly. Not only reasonable but routine.

I mentioned a blue silk elbow cushion. "What!—a blue silk elbow cushion on a mission station in the jungle?" I answer, "Yes, a blue silk elbow cushion is just as comfortable in a jungle as in an American city." If you have a silk-elbow-cushion personality, it is not necessary to develop a barrel personality in order to be a successful missionary. Your normal life when surrendered to God will be preserved by Him through any experience into which He leads you. You can go to the very ends of the earth under the orders of a living Christ, and there spend your days under circumstances that try you to the utmost, yet come back with a faith more triumphant and radiance more beautiful than when you ventured forth. Indeed, the finest quality of inner radiance comes only from those who in difficult places or circumstances have at great cost walked with their Lord. It is that intimate acquaintanceship with Him when the pressure is on that produces a beautiful and fragrant life.

The servant's path should be no smoother than his Lord's. Did not Jesus leave His ivory palaces and enter a "world of woe" by way of a manger in a stable? Did He not often walk with weary feet the dusty roads of earth? Did He not hammer and saw at a carpenter's bench? Did He not wash men's feet? Did He not sit on an old well curb and request drink of a stranger? He even took men's spittle. At length from that Cross which was His throne, He returned to glory and sat down at the right hand of God, still the royal Son of the Father who had said, "This is my beloved Son in whom I am well pleased." If such condescension and exaltation were His, should it be considered strange if something distantly analagous to these should be yours? His personality enthroned within will deliver you from pride, ease, or even from the danger of becoming peculiar and queer. That Person, living within your heart, will recover lost souls on the trail. To surrender our lives to Him for service is the normal thing to do.

The barrel must not arouse self-pity. Permit yourself at least one grand parade in the contents as they come, then make your attack with shears and needle. Deep in the jungle I sat down to dinner one night in a black sateen formal dress which was set off with a strand of red glass beads. The finery gave a lift to my morale, pleased my husband, and thoroughly delighted the Indians when they arrived for the night class. One of our safeguards against the barrel was a family rule that we dress for dinner—regardless. This did not mean formal attire, but it did mean special preparation for dinner. It was good for us.

There are many ways of keeping life normal. A sprig of mint on the edge of your gourd drinking cup, and candles on the birthday cake help. Of course the candles will be there only if you had the foresight to put them in your trunk before you sailed. And really, the ingredients of the cake are not too important—it is the candles that count.

When a government official caustically comments that you are wasting your time, that you might as well go back to civilization, because these savages are at heart no more than the beasts of the jungle, tell him you love life in the jungle, you love the forest people, and you intend to stay right on. You will find it easier to say this with a smile over the edge of a thin blue china tea cup. We did just that, and I know the blue cups helped.

Again you are surprised. "Thin blue china in a jungle!" Well, I might just as well break down and confess. It happened this way. I was in Lima, preparing for the take-off into the jungle, when it occurred to me that I had nothing pretty to take along. Before leaving the homeland I had disposed of most of such things, and only a few very special small gifts remained. When we were forced to remain on the coast for some months, my innate desire for pretty things caused me to covet some of the lovely blue china tea cups I saw in a store window. I wanted them, but I could think of no reason for getting them, except that it was my husband's birthday. So I gave Ross a dozen blue china teacups for a birthday present.

When a little later my own birthday came around, my husband gave me a handsome hand-saw for my present. That is how we happened to take lovely blue china and an exceedingly useful hand-saw to the jungle. We built a tea table, and now on our veranda overlooking the river we could drink tea and persuade army men that we were very happy in our jungle work, and that there were things they could do to help us. On more than one occasion they granted our requests.

MOON MAGIC

T HE TROPIC night drops suddenly, and frequently the quiet is rent by a five-toned wail that creeps across the senses as on pronged treads. I have felt my body contract as my mind sought to analyze the sound I not only heard but felt.

When we seek an explanation of the Indians we are told that it is the wail of a lost soul. We shrug cynically, and inform them it must be a night bird. They in turn shake their heads vehemently and declare that we mean well enough but we just do not know. When we have been in the forests longer we shall know as they do that it is the wail of a lost soul. It is utterly impossible for the human voice to imitate the sound which starts as a shrieking moan in a high off-tone and slithers down to a bewildered lost chord. We argue with ourselves that despite the convictions of the red men it is only a night bird taking the stage in the darkness for a solo rendition of a tragic drama.

We stood, my husband and I, at the top of the river's bank, and watched a large dugout canoe as it moved from the mouth of the branch river, turned toward our port, and nosed into a mooring. The arrival of a canoe from that river branch could mean a number of things. It could be men bent on extending us a welcome, or it could be angry warriors come to tell us to get out—or else. It might mean that someone was dying, or that someone was about to be born. We waited and watched.

Men lifted a woman from the dugout and half carried and half dragged her over the river's bank, then dropped her in a groaning heap at my feet. I had never seen her, but I had seen the Indian Sanquinchi, who was the leader of the group that brought her. He had been at our campfire many times, always listening to our talk but giving no indication whether he believed or rejected our testimony.

The woman was dying, and when I saw her condition I said to the man, "Sanquinchi, why have you brought this woman to me like this?" There was a challenge in his black eyes, and a plea in the lift of his muscled shoulders, as he said, "Señora, I thought if I could just get her here before she died, you would save her." Sanquinchi had seen many wonderful things take place at our post—wonderful, at least, to him—and he believed that I could make his Maria live. She was his wife, and you could see she had once been beautiful. But now beauty had fled before the advance of the mortal enemy.

There was nothing in my kit that would make Sanquinchi's Maria live. There was nothing my hands could do to hold life in her body. But I instructed the men to place her in the palm shelter near my quarters, with the assurance that I would do what I could for her. At least I could make her bed comfortable, and to some extent alleviate her suffering. While I might have no cure for the Campa woman's body, I did have a remedy for her soul. And that, after all, was of far more consequence. For her body would experience death sooner or later anyway, but now that she had come to me her soul need never die. I could tell her of a Name with power to save her eternally.

In that little palm shelter I bathed her body, clothed it in soft garments, and trickled nourishment into her hungry throat. All the time I was telling her the Name that could give her peace and eternal life. But she was not hearing it; already she was past comprehending. I thought that perhaps before she died she might regain consciousness, and that if I were there she might hear the Name. I felt that if she could only hear it, saving faith might yet be hers.

For five days and nights I scarcely left her, as I eagerly watched for some spark of intelligence. But she never heard. On the night of the fifth day, as the full moon crept over the wall of forest that enclosed our little clearing, we witnessed a strange performance that seemed in some way related to the rising moon.

That dying heathen woman, despite her weakness, arose and stood poised on the woven mat. Even as we watched from the river's bank, she stepped from beneath the palm roof into the open moonlight, and began to make her way along the path toward us. Sanquinchi followed, as did her daughters and the others who had either accompanied her or had arrived in other canoes on succeeding days.

In single file they silently followed Maria, who turned just before reaching us, and took the path along the top of the river's bank until she fell exhausted to the ground. Sanquinchi quickly built a small fire at her feet, then seated himself near her head. The others took a similar position in scattered formation near by.

There in the chilled though tropical moonlight we became eye-witnesses to one of the weirdest ceremonies we had ever known in heathendom. Maria began the death chant. Starting with a trembling, penetrating plea, her voice rose higher than I had supposed a human voice could go. Off and out and up, until it seemed to break, and murmuring plunge into the depths. At the lower end of the scale she caught her breath in a convulsive sob, then once more carried the call up and up until it broke and cascaded into a trembling whisper. My nerves could scarcely stand it, and I almost hoped that each sinking wail would be the last. I drew Seroya the daughter aside to ask what her mother was saying, what she was doing. Leaning her slight weight against me she replied, "She is calling for help. She is trying to hold death away."

Maria died, with her call for aid choking in her throat. She had received no answer. I reached into the pocket of my smock for my Testament. Did it not say, "Whosoever shall call shall be saved"? I opened the little book and spread it on the ground near the fire at the woman's feet—a fire that was dying now, at feet that were cooling now. Together, my husband and I read the thirteenth verse of the tenth chapter of Romans. Yes, the verse said, "Whosoever shall call . . ." But it also said, "Whosoever shall call upon the name of the Lord shall be saved." We knew that, too.

Kneeling there in the chilled silence we read the rest of the chapter. "How then shall they call on him in whom they have not believed? and how shall they believe in him of whom they have not heard? and how shall they hear without a preacher? and how shall they preach, except they be sent?" To this we added one more phrase—"except they be sent in time."

We could have gone to the field sooner if we had known that the Campa Indans were totally without knowledge of the Name of Jesus. As soon as their need had been presented in our hearing we had gone. But we had gone too late to get that Name to Maria. She had called loudly and pleadingly, but she knew not the Name on which to call. It was tragic but it was true. We had lived in heedless ease a year too long.

Sanquinchi, Seroya, and the others knew that Maria had

called on a god who could give no help. But they clearly heard the Name we had tried to whisper to her, and they took it not only on their lips but into their hearts. That Name became a shield behind which they were safe, a fortress in which they were secure, a sword with which they could conquer, a sure hope for the soul.

TRAIL FRIENDS

FRIENDS ARE not easily made on the trail. Confidence must be won; it is never offered. We had never seen big Moreno until he came to the camp for the Christmas season affair. A feast is annually planned for this event, to which the entire forest population is invited. The invitations are carried for weeks on the lips of every hunter and other person who touches the mission, and thus goes up this river or that, and across the jungle paths. To each such gathering come those who are attending for the first time. Moreno was one of these.

Moreno had never heard any of the stories we repeated throughout that day. Never before had he felt the friendship that marked the mingling of this unusual throng about the campfires. Large groups and friendly concourse are not the usual order among the Campas. Their savagery forbids this. Generally you find small gatherings at scattered campfires, and especially the Indians keep a suspicious eye on the tribesmen from distant parts. Frequent raids are made on campfire groups. The stronger men are killed. Then the women, children and remaining men are added to the subjects of the conqueror. Under such practices, friendliness is for the most part impossible. It is, however, a quality that even depraved human nature reaches for, and red men proved no exception.

Moreno quite evidently reacted favorably to the contacts made that day, but he did not understand the teaching. I had used charts to explain the meaning of Christmas and various Christian doctrines, and had told the story over and over throughout the day.

At the dinner, a most interesting event, we had seventy guests. For days before the feast our Indians had hunted and brought in their prey. I chose the cuts I wanted for roasts and barbecues and prepared the other parts in their own style. Their ways were not so terrible—just different, that was all.

For this Christmas festival we had imported a barrel of twice-baked bread. Considering the distance, it stood the trip very well and was a rare treat to the natives, for there is no bread in their world, or anything like it. They have no baked grain preparation of any kind. We also imported rice for the dinner. That too was a luxury for them, for they never get it except at this feast. Green bananas were roasted in their skins under the coals of fire, and the root of the yuca tree was baked in its bark. Altogether, the feast was good and the fellowship fine. The teaching was eagerly received by the converts, but the newcomers could only register wonder.

When the crowd was scattering that evening to go to the various campfires among the converts who now lived in the clearing, I placed the hand of Moreno into the hand of Miguel and suggested that Miguel take his companion to his campfire and tell him once more the story I had repeated over and over throughout the day. Obediently that night those two sons of the forest threw themselves beside the fire and rehearsed the things they had heard. And in the morning they came down river together and over the bank to my fire. In no time at all, Miguel placed Moreno's hand in mine, informing me that Moreno wanted this morning to become a Christian.

I have never claimed Moreno as my convert, for I think he was already won before he left Miguel's campfire. There was something about the light in his eyes, and the expression on his face, that told me as soon as I laid eyes on him that he was a new creation.

The following day the hunter returned home. He had not left his camp in order to visit ours, but to follow his usual search for food. It was only after encountering one of the hunters that he had accepted the invitation to come to the celebration. On reaching home he discovered that during his absence both his wife and her new-born babe had died. For self-protection the two boys and their little sister had pushed the bodies into the river; they were afraid that a leopard might come to their camp during the night. In perfect terror they had awaited the return of their father, who had been gone from his camp for several days before he stopped at our clearing. At once he gathered them up and brought them to the mission.

Moreno worked and purchased some yards of yellow muslin and overall material. One day he came to me with a whole outfit of boy's clothing cut and roughly sewed together. Where he got his pattern I do not know, but he had fashioned the various pieces in the style of the garments worn by my son. Hesitatingly he asked me if I would run over his stitches with my sewing machine. Would I? How could I refuse to honor his crude but loving attempt?

Moreno left the station one day only to return some time later with a big Indian he called Nicola. He brought the stranger to my veranda, saying that Nicola wanted to meet the señor. I informed him that Ross was out in the woods, but that he would return at noon. If his friend would wait, he could talk with the white man. That did not seem to satisfy. "No," Moreno said, "Nicola did not mean he wanted to meet the white man, he wanted to meet the Señor of heaven."

We introduced him to the Lord of heaven in the best

way we knew how. We showed him the word pictures of Jesus in the Gospel narratives, as that is really the best way to show Him to anyone. We introduced Him by telling things we knew about Him and we sang songs that introduced Him. Then we invited Nicola to remain at the mission station. He really had nothing else to do so he stayed, and attended our classes. He learned, though not too rapidly. But the day came when he really met the Lord and accepted Him not only as the Saviour of his soul but the Lord of his life. He soon became a good student and an excellent Christian—all because he had met the Señor of heaven. And he had met the Señor of heaven because Moreno had brought him to the mission— Moreno, who had been won by Miguel. How the chain extended! Friends were made by other friends.

One evening at sunset a chief sat by his campfire with his wife, Miguelina, and their little son, Miguelito. Suddenly they were surprised at the sight of Vishu coming over the river. This Vishu was the leader of a bandit group whose violent business it was to capture the women and children of a tribe and sell them into slavery.

The chief was powerless to defend his wife from Vishu and his horde of raiders, so the hapless Miguelina found herself taken to the river, thrust into a dugout, and paddled away to a distant place. When taken ashore there, she found other women captive like herself, lying like logs on the river bank, bound head and foot with sinewy vines. The new arrival brought the slashing of the thongs and release. The women by day were herded like cattle and driven along the jungle paths, then transferred into dugouts and floated along the river by night. This continued until the party was beyond tribal territory, at a point where captives could be disposed of through the bandit system of trade.

On the bandit trail Miguelina observed that when small children faltered and fell back, Vishu would heartlessly shoot the laggards with an arrow and leave them on the trail to be devoured by the hungry leopards. To deliver her son from this fate, Miguelina would gather him up in her arms and carry him for hours. Then, after some years, Miguelina and her son escaped and returned to Campa territory.

It was not until Miguelina returned to her homeland that she discovered the mission station. She sat at our fires, heard the teachings, believed the message, and became a Christian and one of my finest women helpers. Not only did she support me whole-heartedly in the work but she seemed to have an uncanny way of getting answers to her prayers.

One day I heard a lot of confusion. When I rushed to the front of the house I could see a balsa raft approaching from up river with nine occupants I had never seen before. It was no novelty for such a group of newcomers to visit us; it was what we wanted and was to be taken in stride as part of the jungle day. So I paid no special attention to this group until I realized that something was wrong. For the nine strangers were forming a line. I soon learned that the leader was none other than Vishu, who had unexpectedly come face to face with Miguelina, the woman he had treated so cruelly.

In that land when enemy meets enemy the old score must be settled. Campas have memories like elephants, and never forget an injury. No matter how long the cause may have stood, it must be reckoned with when enemies meet. The issue is quickly drawn. Friends of the wronged fall in line on the one side; friends of the enemy on the other. Then the two lines arrange themselves back-to-back, while over their shoulders the leaders call out the terms of settlement. They shake their garments, stamp their feet, and try to reach an agreement without facing each other. It is an excellent method, for often it is the antagonistic look on the enemy's face that makes agreement difficult. If after prolonged harangue no solution can be found, at a given signal the two lines turn and fight it out with bows and arrows. When the fight is ended there is no question as to the decision for the evidence is there. Always the fighting is vicious and many die.

I was curious to see what Miguelina would do, now that opportunity for revenge had so propitiously come. Certainly she had the advantage, for her friends outnumbered those of the enemy many times over.

Miguelina's chin lifted a little as she announced that she would not take advantage of the situation. It was under the circumstances an extraordinary declaration, for if the red man loves revenge, how much more does the wife of the red man! With rare grace Miguelina stated that she would not avenge her wrong, for she had learned to pray, "Forgive us our debts, as we forgive our debtors."

To her this was no idle petition and promise. Rather it was a condition. Since all her debts had been forgiven by a merciful heavenly Father, she ought likewise freely to forgive. And if she did not forgive Vishu, she felt that she could not in good conscience ask God to forgive her. Therefore she would forgive Vishu, and she did.

Prayer, pledging a vow, and the lofty ethics of the Sermon on the Mount, are taken seriously in that land to the south. And a way of life beautiful to behold results.

Vishu and his men had intended to remain at the clearing long enough to earn some knives and other small articles. They did not know it was a mission station. But this unusual turn of events caused them to change their plans and leave at once.

As they climbed once more onto their balsa raft to go down river, Nicola, who had met the Señor of heaven because Moreno, won by Miguel, had brought him, accompanied them, and for two whole days floated with them downstream, explaining more fully the power that had made it possible for Miguelina to forgive, not inflict vengeance. It required five days of hard work to pole his way back.

WHIRLPOOL

The sun chinned itself above the dark, while red men screamed a welcome to their returning god. Christian Indians worshiped at sunrise, then heathen and Christians alike took orders for the day's work, and attended school until noon.

This morning the wicked Preshico had only five of his wives with him. The other was ill. He told me that her infant would arrive that morning; that was why she remained at home. Her house was one of six palm-leaf bowers which were set in a semicircle about Preshico's campfire. The family did not reside in the mission clearing, but up the river and back in the forest. They wanted to seclude themselves where we would neither see nor hear them, for they lived in a heathenism of horrible pattern. Even though they worked for us cutting jungle, we seemed to exert no influence over them.

Perhaps Shangori's need would be my opportunity to gain her confidence. If I could benefit her body, later I might help her soul. I would try. Shangori was the ugliest but best loved of all Preshico's wives, the queen of his household. If I could win her perhaps I could win the entire lot.

A trip to Preshico's camp could prove dangerous for there was no way of determining his reaction. It was merely because he wanted our knives, salt, and harpoons that he worked for us and had all his wives work for us, but when the job was done all contact was broken.

I knew that Preshico would not be at Shangori's fire this morning, so I put on my riding togs, took my knapsack with its supplies of olive oil, absorbent cotton, and a few simple instruments and remedies, strapped a pistol to my belt, and started out. I had never gone to her home, but knew the spot where the path left the river for their camp.

My weapon was that wonderful Marble which is shot-gun, rifle, and pistol all in one—marvelously light, compact and true. It went with me almost everywhere, for danger always stalked the forest. How did I know but that there might be an ugly snake coiled on the narrow path? I could avoid such a snake in the daylight, but if I returned after dark, the knowledge that I had left an enemy on the path would make my return more difficult. Or an inviting small animal might come within reach and thus assist in my shopping for the next meal.

I found Shangori alone with her newly-arrived baby. The welcome in her dark eyes was sincere as she yielded her torn body to my hands. This was her first-born, and his boisterous arrival had been most unkind. There was much to be done for the mother, but when that was completed, I started on the infant. I soon discovered that my half-pint of olive oil and roll of absorbent cotton were insufficient to remove the ashes and black smudges made by the piece of burning charcoal Shangori had used as surgical shears. But I tenderly wrapped the tiny body in oil-soaked cotton and left it until the next day.

When the Campa returned to his camp at sunset, Shangori was alive and so was her baby—perhaps because the white woman had come to her aid. Preshico was deeply affected—became co-operative, tender. He wanted Shangori to live and he wanted her child. During the next two weeks I visited his camp every day. The ashes at the campfire had proved to be a soft but clinging receiving blanket for the baby, and the fever in the Campa woman's body was stubborn. But of far more consequence, there was a man, six women, and numerous children who were the possessors of priceless souls.

Not the least of the dangers incident to a visit to Preshico's camp was the river I had to travel. On one trip Frank and Viola Reifsnyder, our fellow missionaries, went with me, helping to paddle the dugout up the river. We tied it to a tree where the path began its winding way into the interior. When after several hours we returned, we found an angry river swirling about our dugout. A storm in the mountains had filled the big river, lifting its waters above the banks.

I was absorbed in thoughts of the Indians, and was also rather tired when we started our trip down river. Before I realized what had happened the back end of the dugout where I was seated was caught in the twisting whirlpool current and slammed violently against a tree that had fallen into the river. I might as well have had no paddle in my hands, for the sudden impact flung me over the log and into the whirlpool, and I found myself at the bottom of the river, a place from which I had little cause to expect rescue. Reactions in shock are strange but sudden. The mind that is sluggishly weary becomes acutely active. In a flash I recalled that it was on the bottom of this same river that five of our Indians had been lost. Never had we seen any trace of them after they disappeared beneath the surface. I also remembered that an eight-ton mail launch had overturned just two bends in the river above this spot, and was never seen again. There came to my mind a picture of those deadly electric eels which made it impossible for the Indians to swim this stretch of the river.

To add to my complications, I found myself surrounded by a network of tangled vines which were like weak coils when I laid hold of them for assistance. After what seemed an endless age, I rose to the river's surface. There were my friends, sitting in the boat. The first thing I heard when my head appeared above water was Viola's scream, "Save her, save her."

When such accidents occur Indians paddle as near as possible to the spot and there remain for a respectable length of time, as if conducting the last rites for the departed. Then they paddle away and never speak of it. The river has been satisfied, and so must they be. But my missionary friends could not blithely paddle away. If they did they would have a difficult time explaining to my husband.

It was not hard to climb back into the dugout when it was swung around within my reach, but we did not talk much as we resumed our way down river. Because of a kind Providence I was not hurt, only wet and trembling. When we reached our port I heard my husband calling, "Ruth, are you all right?" While we were gone he had been led to retire into the bungalow and pray for me—not for Shangori, or for Preshico's group, or for our group, but for me. It was good to be teamed up with one to whom the Spirit indicated the immediate need and exact time for prayer, and who so promptly responded. Sometimes even now I hear the call from another shore, "Ruth, are you all right?"

But that was not the end of the miracle. Within a few weeks a letter reached us in which a woman described a joint prayer meeting in America, where a member reported that she had been awakened from sleep with an urge to pray for me. Immediately she had slipped to her knees and poured a prayer for me from her heart. Another woman said that a day before the accident she had turned off the switch at her washer when the Spirit of the Lord told her to pray for me. Both women said they did not know me personally; they knew only my name because it appeared in their missionary prayer calendar. At that prayer meeting more than twelve women bore witness that I had come before them for prayer during the three weeks prior to my near-drowning, yet none of them had ever met me.

Following the prayer meeting, the women kept in touch with each other, for the calls to prayer continued to come for another week. Then there was a day after which no more calls came. When God had reached down to the bottom of the whirlpool and dipped me up—for I felt that was exactly what He did—I wrote about the experience in a publication that reached my prayer partners in the States. When they checked the facts, they discovered that the day I was rescued from the river was the last day they were moved to that urgent kind of praying for me.

It would seem that God has registered prayer warriors. A registered nurse who does not keep herself in readiness, uniform in order and shoes spotless, does not get the case when the call comes. Some other nurse takes it. Likewise must Christians be ready. There is a fountain where the stains of indifference, prayerlessness and unconcern can be washed away. There is also a way for feet to be shod with a preparation that will make them ready for the warfare of prayer. But not always is there time for these preparations. So there is another place, one where a person is always kept in readiness for answering the call to prayer. God must have registered prayer warriors at home, as well as missionaries who will risk whirlpools and other dangers. Emergencies come fast on the spiritual battlefield.

VIOLET DAWN

WALKING OUT of the east a queenly messenger of light, morning was touched with perfume and jeweled with dew. Against the forest beyond the river flowers cascaded like a purple waterfall. With each stirring breeze hyacinth blossoms tossed a fragrant offering to the day. Branches moved in the woods behind us, wings fluttered and lyric trills staccatoed the warbling of winged carolers.

Worshiping in the forest cathedral, with its azure ceiling windows toward the palace of the King, I was more than ever conscious that He watches the sparrows, employs ravens to do His will, and gives strength to the eagles. I wanted to be no less expectant of His care than were the birds, more useful to Him than they, and in the depth of my being I longed to exchange my weakness for eagle strength as I waited before Him.

I looked again at the flowering vines which clung to the giant trees and dropped their willowy lengths of vivid blossoms, I breathed deeply of the scented air, then turned to my campfire and peeled the yuca root for breakfast. Thus I felt rather than heard the approach of a man who was near enough to touch me. I had never seen him before. As I looked he did not seem so much interested in me as in the knife in my hand. He wanted to know if he could have it. He certainly could not! It was mine. I had earned it. If he wanted one like it he could earn one, too. There was a clump of trees standing near my campfire. I did not want them there, and a knife would be his pay for cutting them, burning the limbs and making lengths of logs for my fire.

He was eager to seal the bargain, but discovered that he could not cut trees on the mission property until the sun was directly overhead. Even then he could not cut them unless from the time the sun was half-way up the sky until it reached mid-sky he would sit in classes. Mariano did not know what classes meant, but he was willing to learn, for he wanted the knife. So far in his life his implements had been only those of stone and bone.

So he sat in clasess until noon. Then he cut trees. He would have cut trees for the sheer interest of using our axe, all pay ruled out. His way had been to apply fire around the tree trunk, hack at it with his stone axe, burn it again, and continue the slow operation with stone until the tree eventually collapsed. Chips flew as he sharply applied the ax, and the thought of possessing a similar one simply enthralled him. After days of classes and chopping he earned his knife, and felt fully compensated with it.

By this time he noted that the missionary was wearing a khaki shirt, and he coveted a shirt. He could have one if he earned it. He could attend more classes, cut more trees, and have a shirt. By the time he earned his shirt he was so interested in classes that he stayed just for them. Reading and writing were becoming interesting, and the stories told by the workers put hope into his heart and gave him the urge to develop into a real man. One day faith came through hearing the Word of God, and Mariano accepted God's Son as his Saviour.

Suddenly the sturdy young Indian recalled a small matter that had quite slipped his mind—a wife and baby son back in the forest. He wondered if he could bring them to me. We told him that if he wanted to cut more trees and make his own clearing adjoining ours, he could bring his people to live there.

Twenty-two days were required for him to reach his family, bring them down the branch river in a dugout, and up the main river to our place. His girl wife, with her baby on her shoulders, followed me everywhere. They made a picturesque pair—the baby with his small legs wrapped around his mother's neck, and his small garment pulled over her head to bind him fast. The girl mother attended classes, and one day many moons later, knelt at the place of decision and accepted her husband's faith while he knelt at her side.

Mariano was sheer delight. He so enjoyed his own life that he spread gladness everywhere. One night I listened to him talking to a group of fellows of his own age as they lay in the familiar campfire circle in the moonlight back of our bungalow. Lying face down, and holding their heads between their palms, they swayed on their elbows as they listened respectfully and intently.

Mariano's talk was prefaced by the astonishing yet almost off-hand observation, "Fellows, since I am a Christian, I don't need the coca leaf." The coca leaf is chewed by all Campas almost from birth, with the result that every member of the tribe falls victim to the habit of using cocain, a narcotic. The click of the shaking coca gourd is a familiar sound at every campfire. A bone which fits the neck of the gourd is plunged into powdered limestone, and then is mixed with the coca leaves in the mouth of the Indian. Again and again the lime is replenished by transferring it on the bone from the gourd to the Indian's mouth. The shaking of the lime gourd, and the clicking of the bone, punctuate conversation everywhere. To do without cocain is unthinkable, yet Mariano was telling the Indians that he did not need it. It was not a matter of compulsion or direction, but of choice.

It was Mariano's day to hunt, yet when evening approached he had bagged no game. To return to the post without meat was serious, for it meant not only that our family would be hungry, but his camp as well. Since in the classes he had been taught he could pray anywhere about anything and get help from the unseen God, he felt that this was the time to try it out. So he knelt and petitioned help. God honored that simple act of faith, for scarcely had he risen from his knees before he saw a *sacha-vaca*, which he killed and thus brought home a plentiful supply of meat.

One night I heard Mariano calling into my bedroom window. He wanted me to come and help him find something he had lost, something that was very important to him and to his camp circle. When I responded, I learned that it was one line of his eighty-six memory verses which had disappeared and they could not sleep at his camp until the missing line was found. It must be fitted into the verse where it belonged for the evening worship at his fire. Mariano, with other men of his age, learned the memory verses faster than the older or younger classmates, and I had devoted extra hours of instruction to them. Since they could not read from the Bible, I had typed verses on pieces of paper and laced them together with crochet cotton. These they repeated from memory more than by literal reading, and if a line evaded them they were completely lost.

When I supplied the missing line, he expressed his joy with that glad laugh which so often rings through the forest. He thanked me profusely, and began quoting the verse with rare abandon. You would have thought he had recovered a lost wallet or prized beagle hound. When he reached his waiting group with the treasured line of Scripture, the others joined in repeating it, accenting it with a merry scale of rising tones which seemed to run upstairs and end with a jump on the top landing. These Indians never go to sleep at any camp where there is a Christian without first quoting all the memory verses they know.

From my house on the hill I could see the sparkling fires of numerous Christian camps where twilight announced evening prayers and peace in an unfeared night. It seemed so good that their dread of the darkness had disappeared, for I loved night when its velvet curtains closed me in. Silver tones of evening birds died down to twitterings, babies nestled against the warm bodies of tender brown-skinned mothers, while silent stars kept their watch from the sky. It was the wonderful evening of a wonderful day—though a long, long day.

SUNRISE AND SHADOW

Victory is sweet when you have worked hard for it. Since victory was ours, song filled our hearts, and gladness was everywhere. The working, suffering, hoping of two long years had brought satisfying results. Former sullen, hating, fearing Indians now were smiling, loving and trusting.

As we glanced backward, quite trivial did it seem that we had gone without mail for three months at a stretch, that there was no grocery on the corner, that garden things failed to appear because ants trotted off with the seed, and beetles devoured every green shoot that did manage to emerge above ground. Of little consequence was absence of telephone and radio, now that a tribe was mellowing and entering the delights of Christian experience.

Women with awakened consciences wanted to dress in clean, proper garments. How thankful I was that I had dressed modestly when they were darkened heathen, when there was no one to care, except my husband and a wild tribe. Psychologists agree that a secret of health, peace of mind and personal poise is not to pretend, not to overextend. If a life is well lived, it is enjoyment to the one who lives it, and an example to those who observe it. Changed women copied my dress as nearly as possible. To help them, I sewed many miles of stitches, and taught them how to make things for themselves and for their families.

Similarly, the men copied my husband's clothing. They liked his haircuts, too, but had a decided advantage over him because they never required a shave. Though we lived for more than eighteen months without seeing a white person, my husband never neglected his appearance. Indians pull out their beards, using matched shells as tweezers. Generations of this practice have produced practically a beardless tribe. Girls perform this service during courting days as a token of affection, and in return the men etch designs on their sweetheart's face, injecting jungle juices which leave a tattooed effect. Many beautiful faces are disfigured with this grotesque designing, but women will fall for anything seemingly if it is the style. And out there such tattooing is.

We have never seen this practice continued by our Christian women. Neither has there ever been a multiplying of wives. When we first went to the tribe, a man had as many wives as he desired, a practice which was considered neither misconduct nor immorality. Some men had one wife; some had a dozen; each was of equal social standing.

Our Christians quickly replaced the usual shiftless, animal-like mode of living on the ground, and wandering about from river bank to river bank, with a settled home life. Proud, ambitious parents constructed bamboo houses, earned cooking utensils, and made small plantations.

School became important to the Indians, young and old; too, the remedies we supplied in time of need were highly valued. How they loved castor oil! Most of us as children were taught by grimacing adults that castor oil is horrid, but the Indians had not been so deceived. They would gulp down all we would give them, then beg for more.

Quinine administered in quantities sufficient to break malarial fever rendered them temporarily deaf, and this naturally terrified them. But some of the more intelligent men who had benefited from it became leaders in the advance of science in their community by recommending it both by precept and example.

When I reached our post in the interior, I declared to my husband that I should rather stay there the rest of my life than to make the trip out again. The ordeal of travel, particularly on the mule trail, had really been rough, and the recollection of it hung like a weight on my nerves. Yet the time comes when nature takes a hand in your decision. For me the annunciation that I was to have another child served this purpose. This would be our daughter! Perhaps she could be born in the jungle, but her brother could not have been, and it appeared unwise to take the chance. We had intended that she should be a furlough baby. The mission board in New York wanted to be co-operative, even juggling dates a little, and upon receipt of our letter directed us to come home immediately. We did leave just as quickly as we could from a place as remote as the interior of Peru.

Out there it takes a long time to get answers to correspondence, and just as long to get yourself out to civilization. So we began planning. A missionary couple who were working in the high altitudes of the Andes on the other side of the range from us volunteered to relieve us. What fun it was having them arrive! They seemed new and wonderful. It was a relief to be able to place our beloved work in their capable hands when we left for the homeland.

In order to avoid the difficult and hazardous return by mule trail, we decided to go out by the river. We had gone in from the Pacific in the west; we would go out to the Atlantic in the east. The western route was shorter, but in this case that old adage which is so dear to young hearts we found to be true—the longest way round is the sweetest way home.

Everything possible was provided for my comfort, the entire sum and substance of which meant that my husband engaged the only stateroom on the river launch. The launch was a small one of eight tons; the captain was Spanish; the crew were half-breeds; and the other passengers a strange mixture of forest and river folk.

The stateroom proved to be a combination bedroom, captain's office, post office and storage room for dishes. Boys washed the dishes on the back deck, brought them in and stacked them on racks opposite my narrow bed, which was a slat shelf with a thin pad on it. The pad was the principle difference between bed and dish shelf. At night hammocks were hung in our stateroom at varying heights from just escaping the floor to just not touching the ceiling. They intersected one another at frequent intervals and were all filled with sleepers and snorers. We laughed, for we were headed home, and lack of accommodations did not seem to matter much.

After some five hundred miles of this, we transferred to a much larger river boat. On this we could set up a screened bed for our son. Evidently we were passing through a mosquito district, for the buzzing pests formed a fifth column under every chair, and opened a two-pronged offensive against our legs. We practically pushed them instead of fanned them away. David's arm fell against the screen as he slept, and when he woke up it looked as if it had been stitched with a sewing machine. There was a puncture for every square of the screen's mesh. I naturally feared malaria and yellow fever, but we trusted that as God had so marvelously preserved us from infection in the jungles, so He would continue to be with us in all the hazards of the way.

While the river boat was large, the beds were only narrow bunks with thin pads as on the launch. Fortunately I had my sleeping bag with its air mattress, for I found it much more comfortable to sleep on deck with a mosquito tent pitched over me. This eased the trip, and at the same time permitted me to place the baby's screened bed alongside under my tent.

A thousand miles down river we changed to a comfortable Amazon River Navigation Company boat, and finished the remaining two thousand miles to the mouth of the river in reasonable if slow comfort. At the east coast we took a British steamer to New York, where we arrived four months before our daughter was born. As it turned out, Marilyn Beth, Little Flower of the Springtime, could have been born anywhere. Nevertheless, we were glad we were home.

METEORS

Refreshed by our furlough, we made a new attack on the jungle. It must yet submit to us and serve us. Easier said than done, for a jungle is not easily mastered. Nothing is ever finished; you do not clear a jungle but just keep clearing it.

On a stretch of level ground where the trees had been felled, dynamite and saltpeter had helped to remove large stumps, but many small decayed ones still studded the plot we had selected as a playground for the Indians. Evening after evening at the sunset hour my husband and I exercised ourselves for an hour in knocking out stumps. This might seem like rather rugged work for a recreational project, but that depends entirely on the mental attitude a person takes toward it. Do we not consider striking a golf ball with a club good sport? Then why not hitting a stump with an axe? It was good discipline as well as excellent physical exercise.

One night I thought the next would see the project finished, for the plot seemed nearly cleared. But when I counted the remaining offenders there were exactly ninety-seven. However, the end was worth all the effort, for the plot has been kept clear and is a fine playground still, in the midst of a fast jungle thickness.

Since we could not mold the climate to our taste, we did our best to keep refreshed in it. We saw to it that cisterns were always full of fresh rain water. These cisterns had been constructed so that drainage was easy, and they were washed down thoroughly every several moons. Even in the dry season there was enough rainfall at the new moon to fill them, so our water supply at all times was plentiful. Since there was no water in the ground, wells were impracticable.

When we returned for our second term of service we knew better the kind of equipment we should take with us. We entered the jungle the river way as we had come out, and thus were able to include many items the mule trail would have excluded. Tickings filled with jungle kapok were replaced by modern inner-spring mattresses. Comfortable beds displaced the hand-made frames to which mesh springs had been hooked. We took a Crosley Icyball, which meant we had refrigeration to change the countenance of jungle life. A cool drink! Butter to be spread instead of spooned! Fourteen ice-cubes every twenty-four hours!

A pitcher pump and a length of hose went with us, so that water could be drawn from the cisterns. My husband procured an oil drum from the captain of the mail launch and installed it in the loft under the galvanized roof. Indians applied man-power to the handle of the pump, transferring soft water from the cisterns to the drum, and a shower attachment brought the refreshing, sun-warmed rain to revive us many times a day. A cement base and drain were easily fashioned, and our children could enjoy the luxury of a shower whenever they wished, and so could we.

It seemed that our new term was to be full of joy, for spiritual growth among the Campa converts was rapid, and success attended our efforts with continually increasing momentum. Of course problems and perils were never too far around the corner. When a *tigrillo* came slinking out of the jungle and stole our chickens, we optimistically hatched more chicks. When an earth tremor overturned our banana groves we sought new shoots and cultivated another stand of banana trees. Again, when a tornado capriciously lifted the roofs off our palm buildings we dispatched Indians into the forest for new leaves to make fresh coverings.

One morning when we returned from classes we discovered against a cedar panel of our dining room wall a finger-wide mud tunnel which began at the floor and reached to the ceiling. We knew what that meant. For protection against termites we had erected our bungalow on eighteen-inch pillars cut from the trunks of ebony trees. Not unlike a medieval castle with its defensive moat, the pillars rested on cement bases which were surrounded by octagonal trenches filled with water to prevent ants from entering the building. Kerosene or creosote in the water discouraged the breeding of mosquitoes. But whatever we did always seemed to demand that we do something more. Kerosene and creosote never reached us at less than a dollar a gallon, yet we had to have them.

Before removing the mud tunnel and ridding the house of the ants, we went outside to determine how the pests were getting in, so as to halt the invasion. Their method was simple. Dust had blown across one of the six-inch trenches in such manner as to construct a causeway. This the hordes of termites used to truck their materials for building the secret tunnel which they purposed to use for a sneak attack against our dwelling.

One night we found the kitchen floor and walls covered with large, dark sugar ants. Before heating water to kill them we sought their port of entry also. Their method too was simple, for an Indian had thoughtlessly left an arrow leaning against the side of the house. The result was that along its length had traveled a whole stream of ants sufficient to have devoured our entire food supply in a single night.

When several of our hounds died almost simultaneously we suffered a serious loss, but when the very next week we lost a German police dog, tragedy really had entered our family circle. For dogs to us were almost indispensable. They patrolled the property with a keen sense of responsibility, notifying certain men that they were not wanted, and showing a rare power of discrimination. They drove snakes away, warned of leopards, hunted wild game with us and for us, at times bringing it within easy range of our guns.

When my husband returned to camp one unforgettable evening I knew at a glance that he had suffered an injury. There had been no accident, but he had worked too hard, been too deeply concerned for the Indians. There had been too many days of drudgery and nights of wakefulness; they had taken an awful toll. From that night on he could not walk quite so far, or work quite so long, without suffering fatigue. We knew he had given too much to expect any reserve for the future; even at the present he would have to go more slowly. Few workers volunteer for such a primitive spot as the interior of Peru, and there would be no one to do his work if he ceased. So, like a good soldier, he did not forsake his post so long as he could work, even though he suffered as he struggled. I would see him begin each day with as much zeal as if he thought it might be his last day on earth. My secret awareness of his injured heart was traced in meteoric pattern deep inside me. The stars of my cosmos seemed to be falling all about me.

KALEIDOSCOPE

THE FIRST dime I ever spent bought a tin horn. The second bought a box of fourteen crayons, but only after I had rejected a glass ball which contained a miniature village over which snowflakes drifted in swirling confusion when the weighted glass was turned over. The beauty and mystery of it made my heart warm and throb with an almost uncontrollable desire to possess it, but I put it down. Crayons offered greater possibilities.

The spheres of our lives, however earnest, cautious and right we have intended them to be, are sometimes inverted by vicious or careless hands. Fragments of colored kaleidoscopic glitter in confusion—yet broken pieces may fall into artistic patterns of exquisite beauty when viewed from the right end of the kaleidoscope. The little world which is our life is sometimes strangely twisted by circumstances or Providence. Much wisdom and patience must be employed while we await the righting of things and the revealing of the destined pattern—even as the little village appeared after the crystal globe had been replaced on the counter.

Guardian angels are perhaps assigned for the full life span of their charges. Preparation for much that I faced as half of a pioneering partnership was provided in the out-of-doors schooling of my childhood.

I remember that the constantly chanting white guinea hen would not lay another egg in the nest if my hand reached into it. Her delicate flesh would turn blue if she were frightened, so she must not be alarmed. With a silver spoon I took her eggs without offending her.

Perhaps a whole week of early morning sleuthing would be required to trail the elusive turkey to her nest clandestinely hidden in a distant fence row, or against a log at the edge of the woods. It must be found in order to bring her and her flock to the safety of shelter, lest a chilling rain or sly woods animal rob her of her chirping possessions.

Here in the jungle I learned from the Indians the secrets of finding the nest of the *paujil*. This great bird lays but two eggs a year, but they are worth finding.

Grafting in our own orchards had taught me that a tree did not need to be destroyed because its present fruit was not pleasant. I could never forget the wonder of the pear-bearing limb on one of our apple trees. Now, in our clearing we grafted precious orange cuttings into sturdy growths that gave us wonderful fruit.

The matched black horses that ran away, breaking equipment and endangering lives, were not sold, but fitted into heavier harness and to weightier equipment to teach them the meaning of service. Training horses, while different from training men, is not far removed in principle of procedure. I remembered father's dealings with the horses as I worked at taming a tribe.

When gypsies pitched their camp in the lane beyond our meadow, they angered my father by stealing several of our young turkeys instead of asking for food, which he would gladly have given them. During the night a rough member of the troupe cruelly beat one of the young women, and father thrashed the man thoroughly and drove the entire caravan away.

Out in the jungle the Indians did not want to own chickens. Even the most intelligent among them were with us for two years before they were willing to submit to the bondage which possessing domestic things involved. When the Campa went hunting he took his wife with him, and she carried everything the family owned in a basket which rested against the small of her back and was supported by a band over her head. If husband collected more items than his wife could transport, he merely added another wife to weave and bear another basket. If he left them at home, the women as well as his other possessions would be stolen before he returned from the hunt, and besides, he would find them useful in carrying the game and preparing his meals. When at length he added his clearing to ours, and planned his own home and garden, domestic life and a settled place of abode began to appeal to him, and possessions were no longer despised but rather desired.

Perhaps my colored crystal world did shatter and tinkle like broken glass when my stalwart partner went pale and weak at the close of the day. He would continue to the best of his ability, I knew, and I must stand a little taller, and take a stride a little longer to compensate for what he could no longer accomplish. I must find the right way to look at this, so as to see the pattern that was forming, and not spoil its progress. I would stand for a while on the river's bank and think through the new demands I must accept, the fresh battles I dare not lose, the banners of victory I must keep flying.

I learned a lot from the river, fresh and strong. Each morning it was a renewed river; its water had never been there before. A whole flood had come down during the night; perhaps the very water that was passing now, through air of desert heat, had been snow in the Andes only a few brief days ago. Yesterday the river was low and still, but this morning it was a rushing torrent. Yesterday it was a silver streak; now it was azure blue reflecting the clouds.

I lifted my eyes from the river and peered across the V of cleared ground which reached to the river branch. There I saw a large purple cross in the tops of the trees that fringed the banks of the branch river. Heavy vines had climbed and spread themselves, and overnight their blossoms had opened to make a perfect cross in purple flower that seemed to be lifted to heaven. A gentle breeze bore its rare perfume to me even as I marveled at the unusual and beautiful sight, a fragrant cross.

Then I thought of another Cross, one that had lifted from the earth the choicest flower of heaven—the Rose of Sharon; the Cross that had lifted the Saviour even of the forest folks out there at the end of the trail. It was the power of that Cross that had brought us out to this isolated spot in the jungle. The sign of that Cross was the guarantee of our victory. It had been the sign of Christian conquest in every age—*In hoc signo vinces*. The broken pieces were falling into their places and forming the Cross—a broken Saviour—His broken Servant— broken hopes, but blended gem-colors as of jasper, sapphire, emerald, topaz, jacinth and amethyst. While it was the Cross, it was also the foundation of the Eternal City. The sunlight of His love shining through my tears made rainbows of them and I knew that, like the river, my strength would be renewed day by day, so that with a fresh supply from heaven's hill I would be a channel to carry living waters to others.

STARTIDE

D USK HOURS are unknown in the tropics. It is day, then suddenly it is night. Our experiences conformed themselves
to the design. Nothing was ordinary, nothing mediocre, nothing monotonous. We lived in extremes. Things were very
good or very bad. Apart from typhoid fever and childbirth,
I had experienced no illness during my eight years in South
America, or in the three years of married life before that, or
in the years of schooling and professional occupation still
earlier. In contrast, childhood diseases had been violent, but
that had been long ago.

Little sufferings were passed over unmentioned. They
would go, and there was constant need of sharing assurance,
giving encouragement, and providing gladness. To be greatly
loved is a responsibility. Selfishness is fecund, but strong love
has its debility. It stoops to pity, then to pamper, and presently
turns to oil and honey instead of wine and fire. Sabotage is re-
grettable waste. I was well and glad to be, to the extent of my
limited ability, wife, mother, teacher, nurse, architect, land-
scaper, exterminator, interior decorator, social counselor, sec-

retary, reporter and recreational director. I did other things, too, not always well, to be sure. Then suddenly I was ill—terribly ill.

This day as on most others, I had labored strenuously with no premonition of danger ahead. At high sun I had been with the Campas; at dusk I had heard my children's evening prayers, told them their bedtime stories, sung their lullabies. The cool of the day found me with my husband and then I was off to beauty-rest for the night. Little did I think when I retired that my feet would not touch jungle soil again for twelve years, but that, to my sincere regret, was true.

During the night I suddenly awakened with suffering so intense it seemed as if I were pierced with a sword. Immediately I suspected acute appendicitis, and that was serious. My husband feared the worst. He knew that death at sunset required burial at sunrise in this part of the tropics; he also knew that prowling leopards made such burial a waste of time and effort. Long since the red men ceased to bury—they have time aplenty, but no strength to waste. In his hour of awful need, my husband looked up into the open sky and cried, "My Father in heaven, what wilt Thou do for me?"

Ross knew the Word of God, and a satisfying portion fell from the Master's banqueting house into his mind and heart: "She shall not die, but live, and declare the works of the Lord." Faith inspired action. Quickly he must get me out of the jungle, up the river, over the mountains, and into the British-American clinic on the west coast for surgery. It would have been far easier just to open the Bible, claim deliverance, and await divine interposition right there in the jungle, as we had on many occasions previously. A trip to the coast appeared to be utterly impossible, yet God was impressing the clear directions on my husband. God had delivered the children of Israel from the wilderness. Perhaps He would take me out.

I tried to convince myself that my condition was not critical, but I knew only too well that patients in my condition generally do not survive, even when surgery is immediately available. So assured was my husband that God was directing him that at once he set about building a stretcher and preparing the family for the journey. Whether their mother went along or not, two little children would have to be taken where there was other companionship. The suffering seemed to intensify as I projected my thoughts into the heat of the day, and visualized the rough trails of the long, slow journey to the end of the river, and the rugged heights which lay between me and the coast. It would be a severe trial to my husband, from whom I should be lifting every weight. Then there were Marilyn and David—children who would now have to endure the dangers we had experienced in fighting our way into the interior. And I would be unable to shelter them, care for them, or even comfort them. Concern about plans for the journey, when not blacked out with pain, snatched me from the nightmare of fevered previews, and restored to me the native instinctive urge to live.

Then a doctor stood in my room. The government had dispatched him with a company of soldiers over the Andes and down the river to Leticia, where there was a boundary war between Peru and Colombia over the important port where the two republics touch. I thought surely he would do what was necessary there and now, and that we would not have to travel. How relieved I felt that I could now drift into unconsciousness, stop fighting and even planning, and sink into happy oblivion until surgery was done. But as I watched I detected the look that tells the nurse as clearly as spoken words, "It's too late."

Outside, he informed my husband that it was far too late. Peritonitis had set in, and would complete its deadly work in a matter of hours. Before sunup it would all be over. Doctor and soldiers disappeared down river, and we turned our minds once more to river and mountains.

The scene at departure was no pagan one; not a whimper was heard from Christian Indians. Rather they gathered about to quote promises from their store of memory verses and sing hymns of assurance. Women kissed my hands, profusely thanking me for coming to give them light and hope.

I was relieved when the stretcher was lowered into our noncapsizable steel boat—a boat we had taken with us for our second term—for I felt as if the jerky steps of the Indians bearing me down the river's bank would snap the last slender thread by which my life seemed to hang.

Ross tucked David and Marilyn between the stretcher and the side of the boat, while he took his place in the rear. Before starting up the motor, he asked the young missionary who had come to relieve us if he would commit us by prayer into the hands of God.

The Christians who had gathered on the river's bank murmured their "amens" when the prayer was ended, while my husband declared that even if the last white missionary should be carried out on a stretcher the testimony would not die, for the Spirit of God would continue to live and work in the converts left behind.

We left our friends standing in the jungle. We left our professions just where they were, and we left our pets. Somewhere along the way we would have to be picked up by a plane, and luggage could not go. Our dogs belonged with the work in the forest, and even Laddie could not accompany us.

Those who took our places thought that perhaps the dog mourned our going too deeply, for when we did not return he set out in search of us. After an absence he returned to the post, only to leave again, each time returning thinner and more restless. Then the day came when he did not return. I could wish that there were another life for such as Laddie. But the life he lived he lived so well that it was reward enough. Wherever and however his life ended, the joy of his loyal companionship still abides in my memory. That would be monument and epitaph enough for him.

As we traveled up the river a canvas covering broke the direct rays of the sun; but the heat reflected from the water literally burned us to blisters. When I looked into my little daughter's face, she detected the despair in my eyes and asked, "Mother, are you crying?" I said, "No." Then she asked, "Mother, are you happy?" I assured her that I was. Then the child reached over and touched my hand, saying, "Mother, you are going to get well." God had told her daddy that her mother would not die, and the mustard seed of faith sprang up in her little heart for me.

Night closed in on us and there was no sand bar on which to make our camp. Since vicious animals prowl to the water's edge when it is dark, we never made camp except on sand bars. For two hours we struggled on against the heavy current of a swollen river, seeking a sand bar. Great logs which were borne on the water that had lifted them from overflowed banks struck our steel craft violently. It seemed to me that just one more log must be the last; more suffering I could not endure.

Finally, Ross decided to tie our craft securely to a tree at the forest's edge, and spend the night in the boat. Leopards would be attracted by the fresh game which our Christian Indians had shot along the way. Nothing would deter these Indians; they must go with us to the river's end, and float our craft back to the mission post. Ross and the Indians kept a fire burning on shore to ward off the big cats, and fired guns when their hungry coughs sounded too near.

It was a night of strange half-earth and half-heaven experiences. Our children covered their faces with their hands to keep out the wet winds that whipped and lashed at us. They made no complaint. We were still a united family on earth; for that we were thankful. The river alternately raised and then dropped the boat; then for variety logs would ram it. I recalled many promises from the Word, but now they seemed all to pertain to eternal life and not life on earth. It was a night of crisis.

When life had ebbed to that flickering twilight which precedes the night, God spoke five words to my heart from His eternal Word, "The Lord he is God." That brief statement pulsated in my heart, sprang to my lips, flared before my vision, and throbbed in my spirit—"The Lord he is God." Of course, that was the Lord to whom we had committed our lives. He was God—of the sky, the earth, the air, the river— God of the emergency—He was God! I breathed more easily. The agonies of physical suffering subsided. Questions which had been flooding my mind needed no more answers. Night was intercepted by startide.

Anticipating the dawn, my husband loosed our craft and we made good progress, while stars faded and the strip of blue above us was lighted with the coming sun. Parrots and macaws, two by two, flew across the narrow strip of sky between the walls of the forest, and we mingled our praises with the sounds of early birds. It had scarcely seemed possible that there could be another morning to sing praise from this side of heaven. But how sweet my children's voices sounded, and my husband's words, how assuring! The attention of the Spanish maid who was accompanying me to the end of the river was unfailing. A Christian Indian girl also had come along as companion to her on the trip back down river with the boat.

A whirlpool current pitched the launch onto a submerged sand bar and demolished the valuable mechanism that was our only hope of finishing the trip by river. We asked God for help. It was no surprise when an army captain who was mak-

ing his way up river with five uniformed men in a canoe saw
our helplessness and offered to take us with them as far as
they were going. The whirlpool made it impossible for them
to travel any further up stream with their launch, and they
had to find thirteen soldiers who had failed thus far to put in
an appearance. The soldiers might have been delayed; on the
other hand they might have deserted. The captain would have
to bring them along, and he would take us with him.

My stretcher was placed table-fashion over the canoe
which was too narrow to receive it inside its walls. There was
no protection, except as I gripped the slippery sides with my
finger tips as logs pummeled the canoe and swung it about.
My husband sat at my feet and gave such support as he could.
A steady rain fell throughout most of the journey, during the
night and into the following day.

When we reached the end of river travel, the captain
found the men for whom he had been searching. They had
tried to come downstream, but their dugout had been wrecked
by a floating snag. One soldier had suffered the loss of his
fingers which were caught between the boat and the log;
another, a broken leg; and two of the soldiers had been
drowned and their bodies lost. Yet there, at the very end of
the turbulent river, we were able to lift our voices in praise
to the Lord who is God, who had borne a helpless invalid
and little children in His mighty hands through a stormy way.

We were at the end of the river, but only at the beginning of the eight-day mule trail. So steep was the river bank
that the stretcher could not be carried over it; this problem
was solved by strapping me to the back of an Indian who bore
me to a palm shelter of this little government post.

Before leaving our home we had often wondered if we
could again cross the mule trail. True, we had come into the
jungle that way, but we knew that the government would
not permit anything wider than twenty-two inches to be

taken over the trail. The sharp curves and jagged rocks make it impossible for man or beast to carry larger objects, for they will strike the mountain wall, and if the carrier should miss a step, he would lose his balance and fall over the edge of the trail, which in most places is not wide enough for a second footing.

As if in answer to our questioning, words from an Old Testament story gave us this assurance, "I will bear you as on eagle's wings." In our day this would mean aircraft, so my husband asked the keeper of the post to secure a plane for us. The man shrugged his shoulders and laughed. "Why señor," he said, "you know planes don't come here." So Ross decided to carry his case to higher courts, for there is always a higher court for the Christian. He went to a place under the open sky and prayed to God, asking Him to send a plane.

Throughout all the hours of that day he kept his vigil with God, returning only to check on my condition and to supply encouragement. Then he would go back to his post and stand before God in expectation of the advent of a plane. Such faith could not be denied. There was no other way. Just before the sunset hour he spotted a large orange plane flying out of the east. It passed overhead and he prayed that God would send it down. But it passed on, out of sight, was gone for twenty minutes, then reappeared, circled over us, and landed. When the pilot, a red-headed North American by the name of Williams, was asked the meaning of his strange performance, he said that he had passed into clouds through which he could not battle, so was compelled to return and risk landing at this place though it was only partially cleared.

We knew that the Lord who is God had done this thing, but when we requested the pilot to take us out, he explained that he would not dare do that, for no planes had been used to transport civilians since the beginning of the war with Colombia. He protested strongly that it would cost him his job with the government if he should do so. Then he came to the shelter where I lay on the stretcher, and visited for a little while with my husband and children. Finally he said, "Job or no job, when I fly, you people will be flying with me." So wonderfully did God work for us in the heart of a government pilot.

Immediately a runner was dispatched over the mountains to obtain gasoline, for Red Williams had landed with an empty tank. His supply was sufficient to have made it straight to San Ramon, but with cloud interference he had consumed too much gas. The runner, he thought, could return with gasoline in about three days. Three days! It did not seem to me that there were three days life left in the whole universe.

As the missionary and the pilot conversed, a small plane appeared overhead, flew on, and then like the first returned and landed. The pilot was a medical doctor, now under war measures an air-base official, and flying alone. When he saw a plane down at this place he knew it must mean trouble. So he landed to lend medical aid, and to secure the details for headquarters. The plane was in fact carrying a high official of the Peruvian army. We did not tell him that he had been prayed down. The Word tells us that there are times when we may keep our own counsel with the Lord. It is not necessary for us always to tell everything that is going on between Him and us. We thought this a very good time just to keep our counsel.

The government doctor came with my husband and the pilot and visited briefly beside the stretcher. Then he turned to Pilot Williams, saying, "Come with me." He stepped to his own plane, gave orders to Williams to transfer the gas from it into the big one, then under his orders as a superior officer, to get us to San Ramon before night. The young pilot who had so graciously pledged himself to serve us even at the risk of his job had now been ordered by proper authority to do the very thing he had proposed. Once more we had visible evidence of the fact that "the Lord he is God."

Flying above the mule trail, we snatched glimpses of it from time to time and it did not look at all precarious from a height of six thousand feet. It appeared smooth, short, and like a silver ribbon finding its way through a garden of green tree tops. When we crawled along it down there, we had found it rocky, steep, narrow, slippery, and so rugged it was almost beyond endurance. But from the clouds it was simplicity itself.

Viewed from the high altitude of heaven, earth's pathway one day is going to look like that. How glad we shall be then, if when the way was rugged and narrow we remained true in the path that was ours. How short the way through the wilderness will seem then.

When we were landed at San Ramon we had been in the air just forty-five minutes. How different was that from eight hard days and nights on the mule trail.

The following morning I was placed in an automobile and taken up the mountains to a train which would complete the trip to the coast. Planes do not fly all the way; they are brought over the mountains at a very high altitude, and are not taken out again. For me there was no ambulance service— just an open car. Nor could the stretcher go any farther.

Still difficulties beset us. At the edge of the village a traffic officer stopped us, saying that a truckload of soldiers was on the road, and evidently delayed by some accident; we could not start up the mountain highway until they were off. In that mountain country there is one-way traffic, with cars coming down one day, and going up the next. This happened to be the day for traffic to go up the mountain, and if we did not go today then certainly we could not go tomorrow. Since the officer could do nothing about it, we asked God if He would not make a way. In two hours and twenty-minutes, to be exact, we were notified that the way was clear.

But again we were delayed. For when we reached the top of the mountains where we were to board the train, we were informed that in the disordered state of affairs there would be no train. There had been another revolution on the coast, and in this one the president of Peru had been assassinated. No train had come up the mountain, so no train would go down. Again we called on God—this time to make a train go down the mountain. Ray Clark, who had seen us off from the coast two terms ago, had now come up the mountains to help us on the last leg of our journey. We were all trapped together, but God gave us faith to believe that there would be a way out.

Again we counted the miracles which already had been strung together like beads on a chain to get us this far—a night of safety in the boat, a captain with a will to help and a big dugout to transport us, a large plane grounded where no plane could be expected to land, gasoline from the hands of a high officer with authority to command the assistance we needed, the clearing of the road of interference when we needed to travel it. Surely the Lord who had done all this could also provide a train.

We were not surprised when we learned that some members of the Sanchez Cerro regime had been trapped in the mountains when their president was shot. His fate would be theirs if they did not effect swift exit. When we came across them they were patching together odd bits of train material to make a way of escape to the coast, thence to escape to the islands. If we wanted to ride on a train like that we could just get on; there would be neither conductor nor tickets. We rode on this train from ten in the morning until seven that night. Strangely, it seemed normal and right. I had eaten nothing substantial for nineteen days; orange juice had been my only nourishment. Now on the train my husband fed me bits of apple.

Finally arrived at the coast, I was at once rushed to the clinic. The doctor who had brought our son into the world, a friend and a great surgeon, answered my husband's first question, "Is there any hope?" with, "No, but she *must* live." His superior skill, his gracious concern, and his superb accomplishment I can never forget. The French laboratories could find no explanation for continuance of life under the conditions listed in their findings. It had been three weeks since the appendix had ruptured. The representative of the British and Foreign Bible Society summed up his report in these words, "We recognize the hand of God in the case." To which we added, "The Lord he is God."

SUNSET AND EVENING STAR

THE DAZZLING Southern Cross with its collection of celestial gems is not more beautiful to the seafarer than is the faintest star in the midnight sky to one emerging from total blackness. My recovery from the operation progressed so well that after a short time I was transferred from the hospital to the mission headquarters in Lima, there to convalesce and then return to the jungle post. Just to be alive and spared to my family was a miracle and a joy.

When my gracious hostess asked me to suggest the food for which I had hungered during our years in the forest, I took one look at her table and truthfully replied that there was not a single item on it that I had tasted since we entered the interior. We were just hungry for everything. Lettuce, pickles, and potatoes were my first choice of foods.

I had been out of the hospital only a month when Ross suffered a violent heart attack. On examination the seriousness of his condition was discovered. He would not live more than six months, the doctors said—he might have less than six weeks. It was for us to decide whether we would remain on the coast or return to the States.

Since the first intimation of his trouble in the jungle two years before, he had received occasional warnings that the damage had not been repaired. To bring me out of the forest under such difficulties had taxed him unduly, and aggravated a condition which we had been able to keep in check by following a carefully observed regimen.

We decided it was best to return with our children to the United States. On arrival, Ross accepted the advice of a specialist in New York City and for two years lived in retirement. Then, when no organic improvement was discernible, he decided to follow the dictates of the still, small Voice, and accepted a call to preach in a church near our home. He was warned that such activity would reduce his life expectancy, but he wanted to be useful as long as life lasted, and to serve with as much strength as was given him.

During the two years of resting he devoted much time to prayer for my ministry, feeling that any success which might come would be the result of our combined mission. The more I traveled and told our story, the more people seemingly wanted to hear it, and my time became divided between home and extensive travel in missionary deputational work.

He who gives life heard man's prophecy of six months for his servant and extended it to nine years instead. Doctors informed me repeatedly that my husband's going would not be sudden, that I would have ample time to reach him from any point on the continent. Because of his condition, throughout the nine years of my platform and radio work I was aware that any telephone call, any message, might be a summons for me to rush home. But I returned many hundreds of times with mission completed, to remain for a longer or shorter time before setting out for my next appointment.

The number of calls, and the great distances involved, more and more caused my time at home to be like visits. Always I was received as a wanted guest, and I was treated as

one as long as I stayed. Perhaps families which remain un-
broken and enjoy a healthy anticipation of a full natural life
miss something of the richness which is known to those for
whom life is uncertain.

After nine years of this type of living, our activities fell
into a pattern which seemingly could continue indefinitely.
I found no journey too far to make, no work too hard, no
audience too demanding, for at the end I would be welcomed
home and made ready for a new ministry. A kind of ecstasy
surrounded my life.

Then one morning a few minutes before a scheduled
broadcast, I was informed that my husband had slipped away.
At the time I was on the East coast, and immediately made
plans to return home. I completed the broadcast and started
west, traveling toward the most brilliant sunset I had ever
seen. Sad at heart, I could not but wonder what it was like to
Ross, now that he was on the other side of it. It seemed as if
the sunset might be especially radiant in welcome for his first
evening there, for everything had always seemed brighter
where he was. The gold, silver, purple, and crimson curtains
concealed from our eyes the glory of that scene which was
presided over by the Ancient of Days. I had been left out.
Moses and Elijah, Abraham and Isaac, Stephen and Paul—and
now Ross. On this side it was so dark. The sand was slipping
through my fingers and under my feet, but I rested in that
comforting shelter which true love provides—because stars
always shine.

Ross had suffered a severe attack, and his physician
recommended an oxygen tent for the night. At the hospital
he chatted with his brother-in-law and David until visiting
hours were over. Then extending his hand through the flap
of the tent, he asked our son to offer the evening prayer.

When David answered the telephone call from the hospital early the next morning, Marilyn knew from his responses

that her father had gone. She wept, but David, taking her in his arms, consoled, "This is nothing to cry about. Daddy is with his Lord." The heart of each was comforted at this thought, and when I arrived they shared their resignation and peace with me.

Ross had preached in his pulpit on Sunday, and on Thursday morning was with the Lord. We would not weep unduly or too long. Rather we would try to pick up the threads, to carry on, to live as radiantly and serve as faithfully as had he.

Once more, now of necessity, I went forth to glean, for I had two children to support and educate. Ruth of sacred history received the recompense of a full reward because she combined faith with work. Did not Boaz let her glean in his harvest fields, love her, and make her his own through the rights of redemption? From this love came Obed, forebear of King David, and later David's Son, the Redeemer of the world. I was soon to learn, if indeed I had not already learned, that service in the harvest fields under the wings of the Most High is full-time occupation. When we abandon ourselves completely to the Lord of the harvest, He throws His sheltering garments around us, even as Boaz covered Ruth with his skirts on the threshing-floor. Out of such a love-life of service will spring many Obeds to continue our work after we have been lifted beyond the stars, or our steps have slowed on the paths of sand.

LODESTAR

GROTESQUE DUNES deform the wave-scalloped shore, but they will be gone tomorrow. One cannot chart his course by shifting sands. During the first year that I walked alone I received invitations to take up varied occupations—attractive, remunerative, flattering, even coaxing. Friends assumed that I would change my way of living and method of working, that I would cease my gypsy wanderings over the face of the earth—wanderings which restricted me to a travel case and typewriter, the one that I might be clothed, the other that I might record the thoughts which came to my heart and prove helpful to others. It seemed to be taken for granted that I would either accept an office position or find shelter with one capable of providing for me as I retreated into home and garden.

But the Morning Star had risen on my horizon, and having advanced toward it, I could not find it in me to anchor my roots in the earth. Then, too, there was no time. *Our* children were now *my* children; I must put them through school. And my Indians were still there; I must do what I could to see that they heard the Good News and that they received some of the benefits which accompany salvation. My partner had died for the Campas; I would live for them. I would describe the conditions and needs of the field, and convert my life into a channel through which supplies could flow. People at home who were not called to go must accept, not shirk their responsibility. They could pay and pray. I would challenge the hearts of young people and recruit them for divine service. All this would I do, God helping me.

David graduated from high school in June, and since Uncle Sam would not tap him on the shoulder until December, he could go with me on a tour of the mission fields of South America. This would be an education for him and a refresher course for me. When he was only five months old I had taken him into the jungle. Now he could take me.

We found that to obtain permits to enter some of the South American republics was very difficult, but after much effort one day the last needed document came. I called David to come; we were leaving for South America. Marilyn was to stay at home, continue her schooling, and forward our mail. In her first letter she reported that David had left half of his hamburger sandwich on the steak oven in the back garden where he was doing a repair job when I called.

A few mornings later we stepped from our plane onto the soil of Colombia, South America. There we spent an entire month, seeing things and going places, and making pictures for future missionary lectures. The next month was spent in visiting the Spanish cities, Indian villages, churches, schools and modern governmental projects of Ecuador—places and things I had never had time to see before. Here we saw and learned so much that it was hard to leave; opportunities and beauties were well-nigh irresistible. We flew on to Lima, holding a permit which did not allow much permitting. We were alloted only forty-eight hours, although we had tried to have this changed while we were in New York, and at other points along the way.

Resident missionaries told us that to secure permits for a longer stay was hopeless, nevertheless they accompanied us to the consul. I told him briefly of our mission post in the interior, and of my desire to return there for a visit. After listening intently, he jotted down something in the big book on his desk and told me to go ahead. All he asked was that we report back to his office when we returned to the coast and remind him of the notation in his book.

When we went to purchase tickets for our flight over the jungle, we were informed politely but firmly that the service had been discontinued. There was nothing we could do but return to the two missionary couples stationed there, and ask them to join us in prayer that God would supply us with a plane. When we arose from our knees, Rev. Paul Roffe, the missionary who had been in the jungle when I had been carried out on a stretcher, said, "Ruth, the last time you crossed that jungle it was on a plane God sent in answer to your husband's prayer. Ross is no longer here to pray for you, but we shall trust with you."

We immediately set out by car for San Ramon, the place from which a plane would fly if there were a plane to fly. The airline captain was in his office, and to him we quickly poured out our story and petition. Almost breathlessly I awaited his reply, and a startling one it proved to be. "Señora," he said, "you don't remember me, do you?" I tried my best but had to admit I did not. Then he reminded me that when we were laboring inland he and his wife had gone down river in a motor boat which capsized. My husband had saved both their lives, then I nursed them back to health, supplied their needs, and kept them until they were again able to travel. The young man David was but an infant then.

He told us that while officially there were no flights and

no gasoline, yet tomorrow morning a plane would be ready to take us to our destination, and would return for us ten days later.

I had often wondered how I would feel when I once more climbed over the river's bank and entered the bungalow which Ross and I had helped to build with our own hands, and where we had spent so many happy useful years.

But God gave me strength and grace. That night I slept on the bed that had been mine before the stretcher trip twelve long years before. On the breakfast table next morning were my blue and white lunch cloth, and my salt and pepper shakers. Cashew fruit preserves were in the cut-glass dish I had received from Aunt Anna as a wedding gift. My books were on the shelves, while the outline of the last sermon my husband preached in the jungle was in his Bible. My records, pottery, and cooking utensils were there; the missionary was wearing some of my clothing. I had almost forgotten I ever owned these things.

The missionaries now on the station did not need to be sent out from home when our places had suddenly to be filled, for already they were in Peru, but a thousand miles nearer the East coast. They had responded in our hour of need and had not returned home in all the intervening years.

What a joy it was to greet the dear Campas who had been converted while we were there. They were now mature, and, Andrew fashion, had won their own brothers and friends to the Christ they loved and served.

In the attic of the bungalow I opened a trunk which was filled with personal things my friends had hesitated to touch. Once more I held my husband's picture in its ivory frame. I fingered fabrics that seemed to spring to life, and objects that were almost painfully dear. Then I closed the lid. These were things which belonged to another life. I would leave them there. The little white-screened bed in which my babies slept, and white enamel tub—the young missionary's wife would welcome these.

Perhaps I shall never return to Campa land. The work there is in wonderfully competent hands, and I feel that I can do much more for my beloved Indians by remaining in America. Each mountain peak of ministry brings an alluring prospect; each assignment completed seems to open the door to another.

Now both my son and daughter have married and their dearness has doubled. The sky is lighted by a slender moon, and a scattering of stars. The distance between sand and stars is really no more than that between light and sound. When spanned by contentment, that is no more than a few heartbeats.

Once when we were flying across the Caribbean at dawn the heavens seemed so low that we felt we could reach out and touch the stars. Altitude and atmosphere gave us the sensation. The higher we live above the sands of earth, the more we experience the ecstasies of the heart whose affections are set on things eternal. Association with those who live this way, and memories of others who walked a while with us, accelerate our steps, lift our hearts, clear our vision, and beckon us to the kind of life that shall continue beyond the purple and crimson sunset. While our feet still tread the paths of sand, our hearts are lighted with the guiding brilliance of stars.

The older a person grows, the narrower becomes the gulf between sand and stars—if the growing older has been accomplished in God's way. Youth fears death chiefly because it represents the loss of things, associations and loves. Frequently youth is slow in properly evaluating the issues of life.

These are uncertain and precarious times, in which we dare not speculate too much about the future. If that tall man with the white hair and the long staff, who could have been Abraham, or God, was right in suggesting that I would be unusual, it is in the sense that I have been unusually blessed of God with an abounding peace and fulness of joy. My eternity is sure—my course is set. The path I follow is traveled by many star-guided pilgrims. It will be interesting to catch up with them and hear their stories, too.